Adolescents and Their Social Media Narratives

Adolescents are forging a new path to self-development, taking advantage of the technology at their fingertips to produce desired results.

In *Adolescents and Their Social Media Narratives*, Walsh specifically explores how social media impacts teenagers' personal development. Indeed, through unique empirical data, Walsh presents an aspect of teen media use that is not often documented in the press—the seemingly deep and meaningful process of evaluating the self visually in an attempt to reconcile their presentation with their internal "self-story." Nevertheless, as Walsh outlines, this is not a process without its challenges.

Tracking teenagers' progress towards self-validation from the offline stages preceding online exhibitions, this enlightening volume will appeal to undergraduate and postgraduate students, scholars, and researchers interested in fields such as Social Media Studies, Sociology of Adolescence, Identity Formation, Developmental Psychology, and Society and Technology.

Jill Walsh is a Social Media and Education Consultant and Lecturer in Sociology at Boston University.

Routledge Studies in Science, Technology and Society

www.routledge.com/Routledge-Studies-in-Science-Technology-and-Society/book-series/SE0054

Adolescents and Their Social Media Narratives

A Digital Coming of Age

Jill Walsh

Routledge
Taylor & Francis Group

LONDON AND NEW YORK

First published 2018
by Routledge

2 Park Square, Milton Park, Abingdon, Oxfordshire OX14 4RN
52 Vanderbilt Avenue, New York, NY 10017

Routledge is an imprint of the Taylor & Francis Group, an informa business

First issued in paperback 2019

British Library Cataloguing-in-Publication Data
A catalogue record for this book is available from the British Library

Library of Congress Cataloging-in-Publication Data
A catalog record for this book has been requested

ISBN: 978-1-138-67981-8 (hbk)
ISBN: 978-0-367-87632-6 (pbk)

Typeset in Times New Roman
by Apex CoVantage, LLC

To my wonderful children Ben and Maeve, who will know more about this topic than I ever will. I can't wait for them to teach me! And to Rob, whose love and continued support has carried me on this journey.

To the amazing Dr. Patricia Rieker, whose humor, cheerleading, and deep insights were invaluable resources and greatly improved this work.

Contents

Introduction
"'cause pictures speak a lot of words"

In the children's book *Olivia* (Falconer 2000), Olivia the pig and her family visit an art museum, and after looking at a Jackson Pollock painting, with its swirls and splatters of color, Olivia declares, "I could do that in about five minutes." She goes home and actually tries to recreate the painting on the wall, which lands her in a time-out. Olivia really believes it cannot be that hard to paint like Jackson Pollock. One reason this scene is funny is that many of us secretly (or not so secretly) share Olivia's sentiment about modern art: it just looks so easy—all you have to do is drip paint or make lines on a canvas. How hard can it be?

Often in modern art, the finished product does not convey the artist's behind-the-scenes work to develop the piece. Pollock's paintings, which may appear effortless or easy, are in reality quite thoughtfully created. I start with this brief detour into children's literature because I thought of Olivia's comments about modern art often in the course of researching this project, which started as an in-depth study to hear, in adolescents' own words, what the images they post on social media mean to them. And when I first began looking at their images, I honestly had to agree with Olivia. After scrolling through too many bikini pictures, party photos, "duck face" selfies,[1] and clichéd moments of adolescence (in particular those that highlight the social hierarchies and gender conformity that have been so well documented in the literature and in popular culture), it all just seemed so superficial, conforming, thoughtless, and even narcissistic. Although my reaction was different, my sentiment echoed Olivia's: What is of value here? Where is the substance?

But then I met with teens individually to talk about their images, their decision-making processes, and their motivations for posting the pictures, and I came to realize that the images I was dismissing were really important to them. Initially I was far too focused on my judgment of the end product—the image itself—and had no appreciation for how much time and thought they give to their social media images. These are not just pictures; these are tools they use to communicate with others and with themselves. And images are a really interesting medium through which teens can communicate, as they are a way of "telling one's own experience" (Radley and Bell 2007: 369) visually. Thus we can use these images as data to understand the individual (Radley and Bell 2007; Bell 2010). For teens, creating and curating images means simultaneously considering a dual audience—the images are both for the self and for their broader social media audience. For almost all of the teens in the study, these images served to affirm their sense of self. When they create and curate images they assess themselves, evaluate how others will judge them, and then form some opinion about what they see and what it may signal about them.

Herein lies some of the appeal for teens. Adolescence is a period in which we know that the self is in flux, and yet in the midst of this evolution, answering the question "who am I" might be considered one of the most important tasks of adolescent development (Erikson 1980). In an interesting way social media offers an opportunity for teens to try to answer this, and other questions, by serving as a platform through which the developing self can be seen and judged by both the individual and the broader social audience. Looking at only their posted images misses this because the evaluative work is invisible to a Facebook audience simply scrolling through picture after picture. Yet it is a critical component of their investment—both in terms of time and emotion—on social media. As a result, the effort they employ to create and curate images must be considered as an important part of their social media experience. Observing the bikini picture a teen posts is one thing; understanding how that picture came to be, why it was selected, how she might interpret feedback on the image, and ultimately what it might mean for her is another. In my work, I came to understand that the significance of the images is usually not as obvious, effortless, or straightforward as it may seem. Although, to be sure, this is not the case 100 percent of the time; sometimes a bikini picture is just a bikini picture.

This introduction presents some of the theoretical constructs that inform my attempt to make this backstage work visible and also to understand how it might impact adolescents in their path to adulthood. In particular, I will focus here on the concept of the personal fable (Elkind 1967), which I use as a way to think about the story of the self that exists in one's mind. I also focus on Goffman's (1959) work on the conceptualization of a front stage and backstage presentation of the self, with impression management serving as a tool for this presentation work. Goffman's analysis is instrumental in this work, and indeed his dramaturgical perspective informs a great deal of scholarship on social media use more generally (e.g., Tufecki 2008; Walther 2008; Mendelson and Papacharissi 2010; boyd 2007; Hogan 2010; Zarghooni 2007) because his paradigm allows us to think of the social presentations of the self as a performance, which lends itself so nicely to social media exchanges.

A social media primer

Social media technology has transformed daily life in terms of how we communicate with one another, and how we acquire and share news. It has even influenced how we understand and experience social relationships. These changes have been lightning fast. After all, the first mainstream social media site, Friendster, did not even exist until 2002. This cultural change has affected everyone regardless of class, age, gender, race, and religion, although it is important to note that while the broader cultural shifts have been experienced by most, there are significant digital inequalities that exist and should not be ignored (Robinson et al. 2015). Indeed, studying this complex phenomenon in real time is not a simple matter.

In recent years, much has been made of teens' obsessive use of social media, and the popular discussion about its use among adolescents has largely been reduced to defining social media as either a tool for good or evil. And while this work will not engage this debate, there are some aspects highlighted in the popular press that were evident in my data. Much is made of the amount of time that teens devote to social media during their waking hours. Indeed, when I typed "teens addicted" into Google, it automatically offered me "teens addicted to social media" and countless articles abound about selfie addiction and teens' obsessive checking of their Instagram accounts (and, yes, the plural is intentional, as they are often managing multiple accounts with various audiences). While I will not presume to judge what constitutes social media addiction, my participants indicated that social media, which at the time of data collection focused mostly on Facebook (and Facebook Messenger) and Instagram, is an essential component of their daily lives: 19 of the 23 teens who took part in this in-depth study reported in an anonymous survey that they check Facebook at least three times a day during a school day, with no differences reported by gender. As Sales (2016) reported in her study on American girls' use of new media, my participants said that they always respond to notifications on their phone immediately, regardless of the time of day and always check their social media accounts at night. They reported that they check during the day "whenever I have a free minute" or am "bored" and gave me examples such as waiting in line at Starbucks for a coffee, in the car on the way to/from school, or when they first wake up ("good morning selfies" were very popular among some of the girls in the study).

I will leave it to doctors and psychiatrists to determine the impact of this extensive use of social media on teens' psychosocial and cognitive well-being; however, I think the amount of time they spend on social media justifies an in-depth look at what they are doing in this networked space and why they are choosing this space to do it. Over and over again the participants reported to me in interviews that they go on social media because they want to see what other people are doing and whether any of their Facebook friends have interacted with their posts, either in the form of likes or comments. It is a place to see and be seen; an inherently social experience.

Indeed, social media has become something of a sacred social space for teens. As danah boyd (2014) aptly describes, "teens' perennial desire for social connection and autonomy is now being expressed in *networked publics*" (8). boyd argues that while previous generations found social connection and autonomy gathering together to hang out at friends' houses, at the mall, or in whatever other space allowed them to be socially away from the watching eyes of the adults in their lives, this current generation of adolescents is using the public space they create online to accomplish these same goals. Importantly too, this is slowly becoming one of the *only* places where they can achieve this. The adolescents I spoke with are not mindlessly posting things to social media or wasting their lives in front of the computer instead of interacting in the "real world." Thinking of social media this way does not capture all the complexity and richness of their experiences. The teens I interviewed echoed, almost verbatim, the experience boyd describes in her book; they told me that they have limited time to socialize due to the pressures they feel regarding schoolwork and extracurricular activities, and as such, social media is a "lifeline" (boyd 2014) to friends and the broader social world. As one female participant told me, "I mean I don't hang out with my friends except on social [media]. I mean I see them at school and sports, whatever, but I don't really get to spend time with them there." And because social media interactions happen asynchronously—as 18-year-old Samantha put it, she's often "alone in my room in my pajamas" when she's on social media—teens have some space to think through their intentions and process these social experiences, which can be hard to do in a fast-paced face-to-face interaction. Importantly too, they do not see this space as a separate social world. They want to be in this networked space because it allows them space to be together, but they do not conceive of the networked public as separate and distinct from their offline worlds. It is very much the real world for them. As such, the interactions in the networked public should be understood as a component of their social experiences, too.

As a result of this, many of the things we see offline are enacted online too. While there can be differences in the ways that kids interact in the networked space, for the most part I saw teens enact many of the behaviors and norms we see in the offline space; for example, I saw teens follow what may seem like rather rigid and traditional gender norms in their social media self-performance. I also had every teen in the study articulate to me the importance of likes as a way to affirm social position, which can be seen cynically as just a typical high school popularity contest playing out online with a visual count of the numbers. But while those things are there, and we can wish that they were not, the reality is that they exist offline too. Instead, I want to focus on the work that precedes these seemingly surface-level everyday presentations. While I present and describe the work visible on social media—the images and the likes—the real goal of this research is to reveal the work that adolescents do before an image even makes it to the site or app. The early latent (Merton 1957) phase of the social media process provides insight into the development work teens are doing both on and offline. It is in this work that they engage with their personal fable (Elkind 1967) and evaluate whether the fable they see on social media matches with the one they conceive of in their minds.

Adolescence and the personal fable

Creating and organizing images for social media allows teens to put forth a visual narrative of the self. Through my interviews, I found that these narratives change often, and many are deeply personal. In the decision-making moments when teens decide what to post, the images become "micro-evidence" of the teen, to borrow a term from Collins (2000), by which I mean the images become emblematic of the stories they tell themselves and others to explain who they are. For example, if a teen has created a narrative of the self that involves seeing him or herself as an athlete, it is likely that he or she will choose to post a sports picture, as it is something that matters deeply to him or her. As such, this sports picture is a piece of evidence to the audience; it signals to us both what matters to the person and how he or she may see the self.

The personal fable (Elkind 1967; Vartarian 2000) is a useful concept for understanding these narratives that we create. It is a concept that explains how we weave our stories, experiences, and even our personalities together to make sense of our place in the world. It is our origin story. As originally defined by Elkind (1967), the self-constructed personal fable often overemphasizes one's uniqueness and importance. Elkind saw it as an individual and internal narrative that tends to focus on how our story is different from others around us. The fable is really the result of our impression management work (Goffman 1959) and social constructionism more broadly. This will be discussed in the next section.

While we employ the personal fable throughout our lives, it is especially relevant to the developmental and social experiences that take place during adolescence, as this is the age in which the fable starts to become solidified. While the precise age boundaries of adolescence are debatable, and indeed there is no universal adolescent experience, researchers agree for the most part that adolescence is a time of burgeoning independence in which adolescents begin to see themselves as individuals separate from their families with their own judgments, values, and experiences (Harrison 2005; Thorlindsson and Bernburg 2006; Erikson 1980; Dahl 2004). An emerging sense of self is a critical aspect of adolescent development, and indeed answering the questions "Who am I?" and "Where do I fit in?" is some of the most important work that teens do during this period. The fable, then, naturally serves as a narrative answer to these questions at this stage of development.

Culturally we use the age range of 13–18 to define adolescence, commonly thinking of it as lasting from the onset of puberty to its completion; however, life course researchers choose instead to define adolescence as a socially constructed stage (Elder 1975) when we move away from parents towards peer groups as the primary sphere of influence. Erikson (1980), one of the preeminent scholars of adolescent psychosocial development research, was less concerned with establishing the age limits of adolescence than with positioning it as a time of psychosocial internal struggle. He argued that this stage is "only complete when the individual has subordinated his [*sic*] childhood identifications to a new kind of identity achieved socially with other same age friends" (119). Erikson's (1980) definition implies a tension; adolescence is a time of internal struggle between the self of childhood and the self of adulthood, and there is a constant push-pull dynamic between the two until eventually the teen no longer sees him or herself as a child. As a result of this tension, adolescence may be best thought of as a "developmental limbo" (Smith and Denton 2005: 184) between childhood and adulthood.

Of particular interest to my research is the tension that exists between adolescent and adult identities. Adolescents are expected to be mature and responsible, but we do not want them to be fully mature; adult reactions to their more mature content on social media tell us as much. Fine (2004) describes the adolescent cultural tool kit as containing both adolescent and adult strategies, and teens constantly work to determine which set of skills and abilities is appropriate to implement in each context. Understanding what tools are appropriate in different contexts is not something that is always intuitive and clear, and indeed there are many misjudgments in their execution. This is especially complicated on social media because of the context collapse (boyd 2013) embodied in its architecture;[2] while we know that the social context helps determine our presentation of the self (Goffman 1959), social media challenges this notion because we are constantly confronted with presenting the self to all of our social contexts simultaneously. For a teen who may want to present a more adult presentation to certain audiences and a more adolescent presentation to others, this process can be especially confounding. As a result, I often saw teens post sexually mature images in one moment and then appear very childlike in other moments, clearly wavering between strategies of adulthood and childhood, and receiving very different reactions to the two (i.e., comments like "sexy" for the first and "u r so cute" for the latter). In one picture posted by one of the 16-year-old female participants, she posed provocatively in a bikini on a deck straddling a bikini-clad friend's back, while in her next picture, posted days later on her timeline, she is a wearing a fleece jacket, sneakers, has her hair in braids, and poses childlike in front of a fountain on a family trip. She understands that the peer and family contexts require different strategies, although because she cannot separate these easily on her social media, the viewer is witness to the striking juxtaposition of these two images.

To facilitate their burgeoning independence, adolescents focus on "over-differentiation" (Vartarian 2000: 642), that is, how unique they are and how they see the world differently from their peers. The clichéd teen refrain that "no one understands what I am going through" is accurate when thought of in light of over-differentiation and the personal fable. Of course no one understands, because no one shares the teen's internal dialogic process of self-narrative. Personal fable over-differentiation is largely an internal process; it is the feeling that no one "gets" you, which *can* be articulated to others, but often it is not.

What is particularly interesting in adolescence is that this internal focus on uniqueness directly contrasts the external conformity of dress, style, and image composition evident in most participants' news feeds.[3] But while this seems contradictory on the surface, both social conformity and over-differentiation accomplish the goal of affirming the self; we want to believe we are unique while simultaneously we want to believe that we belong socially. Again, while they are trying to answer the question of "Who am I?" they are also trying to answer "Where do I fit in?" Teens strive to highlight the unique components of the self in their internal work and also take steps to ensure conformity and acceptance by their social group, and social media architectures allow them to work towards both of these goals concurrently.

Impression management and the personal fable

When teens present their personal fable, they do so with the knowledge that it will be seen and judged by their social media friends and followers. As such, this presentation requires great care and time. Teens I spoke with talked about selecting and crafting images for their Facebook feed that were both important and telling. They rarely posted images that meant nothing to them. Again, to understand this strategy work I have employed Goffman's (1959) notion of impression management. Goffman evoked a "dramaturgical approach" to argue that we present the self through a series of performances that are audience and context dependent; for example, in the course of one day we may play the role of parent, boss, employee, friend, and spouse. For Goffman, we are constantly performing in multiple roles over the course of the day and each of these roles requires a different set of behaviors. Generally speaking, we know what is expected of us in each role, and we give the appropriate performance. Embedded in Goffman's dramaturgical approach is his theory of impression management. Goffman believed that the performance is iterative: there is the performance, an interpretation of the feedback one receives on the performance, and then an adjustment of the performance, when warranted by the feedback. This theory is readily applied to social media, and many researchers have called upon Goffman's notion of the performance, or impression management more specifically, to explain the ways in which people present themselves on Facebook (see Tufecki 2008; Robinson 2007; Walther 2008; Papacharissi 2009; boyd 2007; Hogan 2010; Zarghooni 2007).

On social media, this process begins with a performance of the personal fable, or a portion of it, anyway, via image creation and curation. Once the image is posted, the presentation receives feedback in the form of likes or comments or some combination of the two. The teen then has a chance to interpret and make sense of this feedback and think about how it reflects, or does not reflect, his or her personal fable. This is important and sensitive work and involves the social media user really putting him or herself out there. This may explain, at least in part, the hold that social media has on some teens, especially with regards to the obsessive checking of likes and engagement in strategies to get likes. A lot of work has gone into the creation of these images. This is not just a question of assessing how people think you look in a bikini. Though peer approval is a part of it, even a bikini picture is tied to the story of the self. Indeed, while almost all the girls I spoke to had some version of the bikini picture, they all had far more to say about these images than just "I picked it because I looked good," although to be sure they are always aware of that as well.

Goffman's impression management theory is also useful for considering teens' symbolic boundary work and their categories of worth. Symbolic boundaries are the "group boundaries that demarcate the limits of groups—or outsiders from insiders—who share common values or common definitions of the sacred, of stigma, or of exclusion" (Lamont and Thevenot 2000: 4). These symbolic boundaries allow people to create and understand in-groups and out-groups, and give people the language and rationale for categorizing the "other," which serves to clarify and distinguish one's own group memberships (Lamont 2000). Cultural understandings, such as habits and preferences, connect us to others in our group (Jacobs and Spillman 2005), and therefore group boundaries will be drawn around common values and/or common interests. Indeed, I saw this often on Facebook, whether it was through tagging images or creating affinity groups. Additionally, and perhaps particularly relevant for adolescents, these symbolic boundaries can be communicated through physical attributes of distinction, such as dress, to solidify group membership (Blair-Loy 2001). And in addition to establishing membership in the group, boundaries establish hierarchies *within* the group as well (Lamont 2000; Wilkins 2008). The teens I spoke with articulated the boundaries that demarcate the social groups as well as the subtle boundaries that indicate the hierarchies within the social groups. While this is often discussed in terms of larger societal-level constructions such as race, class, and gender (e.g., Wilkins 2008), in most cases my participants spoke mostly about social status—although to be sure, race, class, and gender figure into the ways in which hierarchies are defined and configured. In terms of how this plays out on social media, we can literally see group membership in pictures taken or tagged with friend groups, and Zhao et al. (2008) found that college students believe Facebook users with high levels of "participation by others" (i.e., likes, shares, comments) on their pages are more popular than those with less participation. My teen participants did not report such a neat association, noting that you can be Facebook popular, which does not translate to other contexts necessarily, and vice versa, and indeed simply having people write things on your wall does not mean you are somehow more popular.[4] In general, though, they agreed that there probably was a link between participation by others and popularity, however they were more inclined to agree with the inverse statement—that little to no "participation by others" on social media probably means that the person is less popular. While social media does not capture all of their social interactions, many of which they reserve for more private forms of communication such as Snapchat and other messaging apps, it does stand as a visual front stage performance of their social interactions.

So if posting images and statuses on social media is part of a front stage performance, and participation by others can signal social worth, then the performance creates the opportunity for boundary work or evaluation. The comments adolescents receive offer visual proof of their connections, which means that Goffman's interpretation stage is powerful: not only are they able to use the technology as an indicator of their social worth, that worth is broadcast for all of their social media friends to see as well.

Describing our actions on social media as a performance implies that they are not entirely genuine. If we are always managing our impressions on social media, when do we stop the performance? And if social media is a performance, is it just a presentation of some idealized version of the self—edited pictures capturing only the most perfect moments? I argue that while introducing the concept of impression management may make the presentation sound very strategic and planned, online performances are no less authentic than our offline face-to-face performances. Ewing (1990) and DiMaggio (1997) write of the context-driven self, by which they mean that context drives the presentation of the self. For example, in the context of their family homes teens may act very differently from how they act out on a Saturday night with peers. Neither of these performances is inauthentic, they are just determined by the social context. More importantly, even when we are performing, we never see our performances as inauthentic. In this view, there is nothing artificial about one's presentation, and indeed the individual is not even aware of any contradictions that may exist between the performances she gives, because she is being true to herself in each context (Ewing 1990). Additionally, it is important to note that the concept of authenticity is itself a social construction, and working to be authentic can require more effort than being inauthentic. Almost every teen participant spoke to me about how important it is to be authentic on social media, and noted that they are assessing the authenticity of others' performances as well. They work hard to ensure that they showcase their "true" or "real" selves as they interpret them, albeit perhaps at their best. But again, this is not different from what we do offline: no one saves unflattering or mundane pictures for a photo album or to frame for their homes. Rather, we save the memories that reflect our greatest moments; our "highlights reel" as one participant described what he sees and posts on social media.

One would assume that as teens mature and become more aware of their authentic emerging self, they would remove embarrassing pictures, rude posts, items that do not reflect their current personal fable, or things that may negatively influence their performance or signal low social status to others. However, my data supports Walther et al.'s (2008) assertion that unflattering pictures and comments are rarely removed. Some participants reported that they let the negative comments remain because the absence of any feedback is perceived as worse than negative feedback; as one 16-year-old girl reported, no feedback "is like you don't even exist." Others leave embarrassing images on their timelines to document the evolving self; many reported that looking at embarrassing eighth-grade photos can serve as a source of amusement as they look at what a "weirdo" or "loser" they were. It can also be a visual signal of positive growth for older teens. Several teens who were graduating from high school when I met them mentioned how it was a source of pride to look back and see how they had grown and changed since middle school. Evolution of the self, even if it involves some mistakes, is fun to see. Again, the key point here is that the presentation of the self, including the occasional blips and missteps, must be authentic, however teens define this for themselves. They care so much about this because developmentally it is exactly what they should be doing; that is, working to develop a sense of who they really are. What we see on social media then is the work to create, in all contexts, an authentic self. The self in adolescence is perhaps more contradictory and more confusing than in adulthood, precisely because it is emerging. The work teens do to create a narrative in visual images is a powerful component of social media for teens; platforms such as Facebook and Instagram allow them to work through the personal narrative, think about how to present it strategically to their social groups, and then reflect upon it both before posting and after receiving feedback from peers.

The fable goes online

While Elkind (1967) thought of the personal fable as a story that is created and evaluated internally, social media has altered this experience by making the fable public. Though not every image is thought through well enough to constitute part of the fable, and to be sure no one image alone communicates the whole fable, social media provides the opportunity to create a visual representation of the inner self-story. And images offer an interesting way to tell stories for teens who may find it hard to verbalize or enact certain aspects of the self-story in their offline lives; the images can tell the stories for them. As Sara, a superconfident 18-year-old recent high school graduate described it to me, "certain pictures mean certain things." Thus with an image she can signal things about who she is and what matters to her without having to say the words out loud. And of particular interest is the fact that she believes that she knows what the images mean and assumes that her audiences will read them in the same way. To be sure, very rarely did a teen tell me that an image represented him or herself entirely; rather, most images were only pieces of the fable that they deemed worthy of highlighting. But all of the ideas about the self can be depicted if the teen is interested. And in this way, the images he or she posts can be seen as visual representations of the emergent self, which teens hope align with the story of the self they internalize. While a lot of this work is subconscious (i.e., teens do not say, "Now I will show this part of my story"), adolescents do invest a lot of time and energy in this presentation of the self.

In talking with teens it became clear to me that everything happens lightning fast on social media—certainly not a novel insight. However, while the interactions and responses are fast, creating a visual narrative does not move at this same fast pace. Teens reported that they take time to think about a picture and how it will be received before posting it, which is in contrast to responses they send to texts, Snaps, and other forms of communication that require immediate responses. Because they manage their accounts on their own terms, often asynchronously, they can afford the time necessary to think through and craft a version of the self that is both real for them and appeals to others. This is an area for new and future interesting work.

One important note: Throughout the book I talk about how social media allows teens to take the time they need to control their presentation. I am speaking here only of the new images that they post, not their responses to content, whether this happens via texts, comments on other people's social media posts, or Snapchats (Katz and Crocker 2015). Social norms around communication via messaging apps like Snapchat require immediate responses and thus do not afford users the same amount of time to craft a thoughtful presentation. At the time this data was gathered in 2012/2013, Snapchat was not very popular with my participants and therefore it does not factor into this analysis. I acknowledge, however, that these findings are harder to apply to these instant messaging apps.

The research setting and method

I conducted my research in 2013 and 2014, with a few pilot interviews and social media observations taking place in late 2012. This was the time when teens first began migrating en masse to Instagram and using Facebook less. However, according to market data from that period, while teens' interest in Facebook may have been waning, both sites (along with Twitter), remained very popular with teens (Edwards 2013). As mentioned above, apps like Snapchat, Tinder, WhatsApp, and Yik Yak were not widely used by the teens that I spoke to at the time. As such, most of the conversations I had with teens focused mostly on the images they posted on Facebook and Instagram. I spoke with teens from the area around a northeastern U.S. city. The teens lived either in the city or in the surrounding suburbs and attended a mix of public, private, and charter schools. I spoke with 26 adolescents, 13 girls and 13 boys, aged 13–18. Participants were overwhelmingly White; two female participants identified as Asian and one male identified as African American.

I want to explain briefly the methods I employed in my work, as they were critical to my ability to hear about the backstage work in adolescents' own words that became the focus of this book. The methods, too, allowed me to upend many of my assumptions about what was taking place, and more interestingly what I believed these things might mean to teens. Given the methodological debates concerning social media ethnography (see Postill and Pink 2012; Hine 2000) and the lack of available data on young teens' (aged 13–18) lived experience with social media, this work began as a grounded theory exercise, and I had no real sense of whether my findings would support the current theoretical frameworks in the field. However from the beginning I felt confident in these methods because I knew they would elicit a deeper understanding of the Facebook experience in adolescence.

The 26 adolescents (ages 13–18) who agreed to participate in my multi-method research study allowed me to talk to them in groups and individually about how they make decisions and meanings about what to post and also to observe them in real time doing just that. I began with single-sex focus groups, during which we talked about the general trends, the meanings, and also the confusions, they make and take from social media.[5] At the beginning of the focus groups, participants were asked to complete an anonymous survey about their social media usage as well as their perceived physical and emotional health and well-being.

After the focus groups I spent two weeks engaged in an image observation, during which time I examined the 125 images participants posted on Facebook or were tagged in by others. I also observed all of the "participation by others" (Zhao et al. 2008) connected with these pictures—the comments, shares, and likes—that these images generated during this time period.[6] To accomplish this, I set up a dummy Facebook account and friended my participants. I chose intentionally not to include written status updates in my data because all of the teens told me in the focus groups that images are the most important component of Instagram and Facebook. I had no direct contact with participants during this time.[7]

After the observation period, I interviewed each participant to understand the stories of these images from the youths' perspectives. I was interested in two stories: the story that the image intended to tell and the story of how teens negotiated Facebook's social rules to achieve this. The beginning of the interview was focused more on their day-to-day experiences on social media, but to get at their meanings and motivations, I selected several of their images to review with them. I asked participants simply to "tell me the story of this picture," as I wanted to understand both the image and the decision-making process involved. This approach was derived from Becker's (2003) claim that one important consideration of visual sociology should be to analyze how an image came to be. I adapted this approach to address both the story of the image and the story of how it ended up on Facebook (see also Harper [2012]). After participants described these stories, we talked about their reactions to the image and the responses their images generated.[8]

In almost all cases, participants described carefully considered choices; they described thinking through what would happen when an image reached Facebook, both what it would say about them and how it would be received. They talked about deciding what to capture in an image, the logistics of how to get this image, and trying to interpret the feedback they received. And perhaps most interestingly, they talked about evaluating an image as a piece of "micro-evidence" (Collins 2000). From a photo's creation to interpreting friend and self-feedback after it was viewed on Facebook, teens described a thoughtful process. This work was important to them in part because participating on social media successfully is a social accomplishment, a fact that has been well documented in the literature, but also because it provides an opportunity for self-reflection and assessment. If teens are working to thoughtfully present the "real me now" on social media, then part of what they must do is engage in self-dialogue before they even post the picture; they have to figure out what the visual presentation of the "real me" is and looks like, and evaluate how to create or organize images that highlight this. Ultimately, this first phase of the process encourages them to reconcile their online presentation with their self-story—who they think they are at the moment.

Given this new reality of "highlights reel" postings and the constant visual documentation of the "real me" that kids talked about so often, personal fable theory (Elkind 1967) must be altered to account for an unintended effect of social media on the fable development process. The development of the fable is no longer a solitary internal process due to the "prosumption" (Davis and Jurgenson 2011) that is a technological affordance of social media. As teens have the ability to produce content on their own as well as on others' news feeds, they end up both producing and consuming social media, often simultaneously. This means, too, that the personal fable is being produced and consumed simultaneously as well. For example, let's say I post a picture on Facebook that I believe tells a key component of my story. Instead of just evaluating the content I produce for myself, I also consume the content that others produce on my news feed in terms of likes, comments, and shares. Thus my fable is continually being produced and consumed relationally, which impacts the construction process.

A few caveats before moving forward: For one thing, the teens I spoke with reported that, for them, there is no clear division between the public and private contexts of our lives. Jurgenson and Rey (2012) write that it is not a "zero-sum game" in which we exist entirely in the front (public) or back (private) stage with no overlap. Rather, these two contexts are deeply connected, often occurring simultaneously, and very fluid. While we assume that we trade our privacy to offer a public performance on social media, in reality, Jurgenson and Rey (2012) argue, the private work is a key part of the performance, and even "implicated in the reveal" of what we see on social media. This is a critical component of why social media, as public as it is, allows for the thoughtful work I describe in this book. To put it simply, the more public presentation work we are required to do for social reasons, the more self-work we inherently engage in to create and curate the public self. Thus, when I describe the components of a public self or public presentation in this book, it is never the case that the front stage work is without private backstage consideration. And the reverse is true as well; the backstage is always aware of the public effects and experiences of the front stage.

The self presented through images, then, is co-created by the teen, who works privately to post publicly, and then the audience who consumes it and produces feedback. The teens anticipate and want the feedback of others and are always aware of these public mirrors. Through the architecture of social media, the fable is publicly available for assessment for both the individual and his or her peers. This is quite literally "the real me now" as kids work to develop these performances as "true reflections" of the self.

Secondly, I believe teens' micro-decisions about the self can and should be documented and analyzed without attempting to label participants' identities. In fact, while identity is important to this process, I contend that the work is more fluid than what is implied by the notion of a fixed identity (for an interesting discussion on fixed vs. fluid identity, see Giddens 1991; Brubaker and Cooper 2000; Somers 1994; Erikson 1980; Ewing 1990). Thinking only in terms of identity obscures the dynamic aspect of the personal fable work on social media. The data presented shows that teens' stories and the images that represent them may be tried and discarded, or solidified. Although the experiences and self-reflection I document here may someday lead to identity formation, I do not claim to know how this process takes place. Instead, I have focused on how the micro-decisions about the self affect the development of an internal self-story in adolescence.

Related to this, when I talk about the fact that these teens want to be authentic, or "real," as they often call it, I am not referring to the authentic self as some underlying "true" self as it is often thought of in our society writ large. Rather, authenticity is constructed socially. Davis (2014) notes that this notion of authenticity as the "uncalculated core" (6) is an important impression that the actor maintains not only for others but also for the self (see also Goffman 1959). Davis writes that in reality authentic work involves presenting what she calls the "ideal self," and what I term the "highlights reel," in a "seemingly natural way"; in essence it means to "engage in identity work, while hiding the labor of doing so" (6). It is the natural aspect of the presentation that makes it feel authentic. Of course, the focus is on showing our best selves to others and assessing the feedback we get on this version of the self. At the same time, we must ensure that we show our best selves in a way that seems almost effortless. Sims (as quoted by Pascoe 2010) calls this "controlled casualness" to describe the ways that teens can use the asynchronous communication as a way to cultivate an "ideal self" that is casual and appears effortless. The key point is that the authentic self that these teens described to me is still a highly constructed and controlled presentation, it just has to *feel* natural to the producer and consumer of the image.

Because the public and private are not dichotomous, these teens' performances of the ideal self become important to them. They "are not empty signifiers but true reflections of the self" (Davis 2014: 7). This is critical to understand the concept of authenticity as used by the teens in this book. The goal here is not to evaluate whether they are presenting the authentic self on social media or even to try to understand what that might look like for them; rather, the focus is on the fact that the presentation *feels* authentic to them. They see the presentations as "true reflections" of themselves.

Outline of the book

Throughout the book I will show the teens' images and include quotes from the interviews and focus groups. I have chosen not to "clean" the quotes to retain the feel and context of the quotes. I based this on Paget's (1983) argument about the importance of allowing the richness and complexity of participants' voices to shine through in the empirical chapters. Paget presents interview data in complete and raw form, as she believes that "in-depth interviews systematically create knowledge. Their form and content, when preserved, examined and displayed, demonstrate that process" (1983: 69). Paget's thinking on this encouraged me to include longer excerpts of the exchanges between participants and me, as a way to present both the context in which the answer was given as well as the participants' language stops and starts as they work to explain their decision making and thought process. While this can be a bit more challenging to read at times, I did not want to edit their language too much, as this is the first chance we have to hear their reflections.

Chapter 1 introduces the surface self-presentation, or the front stage work, that happens on social media and documents what the teens in the study posted on Facebook. This is what we see, the Goffmanian front stage in which judgments about others are often made, and as such it is an appropriate place from which to begin the data analysis. In this chapter, I introduce several image typologies to frame the ways in which study participants present the highlights reel of their lives on social media. This chapter also addresses peer feedback in the form of likes and comments.

In Chapter 2, I document and illustrate the social rules that guide adolescents in how they present the self on social media. Although adolescents do not discuss these unwritten rules in any specific way with their peers, they learn them by observing others' social media images and actions. Teens do not have to follow these rules, but doing so enables them to confirm their social belonging to the dual audience of themselves and their peers. Thus, the self that gets presented here is bound by internalized social rules. These rules also serve to highlight social categories of worth, separating those who can follow the rules from those who cannot, and offers an explanation for why so many of teens' images are so similar to their peers.

In Chapter 3 I examine how these rules are gendered and argue that besides some universal rules, such as being authentic and emphasizing appearance, social media experiences are gendered in important ways that may have implications for adolescents' construction of gender norms and gender identity. In particular, the importance of affirming masculinity in boys and femininity in girls, which is profound at this age, is exacerbated on social media.

Finally, in Chapter 4, I return to the backstage work to focus on the inner dialogue that the social media performance cultivates in adolescents. I argue that some of the most important social media work happens when teens curate and examine their photographs before posting them. I also elaborate on my interpretive theory of adolescent social media use to argue that the self-reflection social media architecture provides for adolescents is altering their path to self-development.

In the conclusion I outline areas for potential future research. I contend that the story of adolescent social media usage is a complicated but necessary one for us to understand. Regardless of what we think, adolescents are co-opting the technology and using it in ways that have interesting implications for their path to development. We need to understand these processes so that we can understand adolescent development in a social media context.

Notes

1 Selfies are pictures that people take of themselves on their phone.
2 It is important to note that this research was conducted before the popular rise of Finstas (Fake Instagram accounts). My current research suggests that teens are using Finstas deliberately to manage context collapse, creating different Finstas for different audiences, but at the time this data was collected these teens did not have access to this as an option.
3 There are two exceptions to this in the study, interestingly both males—Jake and Noah. Both will be discussed in subsequent chapters, but for now, it is important to know that Noah actively shuns conformity as part of his fable while Jake has made a series of social media missteps that resulted in bullying and subsequently a very generic presentation of the self.
4 While Turkle (2011) found that college students rarely email each other or use the message feature on Facebook because these "will do nothing for your image" (251), my participants refute this, and actually said they utilize the Facebook private messaging feature more often than the main page. Still, I agree that the messaging feature is more similar to a private conversation than the widely visible images or statuses teens post on Facebook.
5 I included focus groups in my research because they afforded me the opportunity to hear how adolescents talk about Facebook in a social context of same age peers, similar to those with whom they interact on Facebook (Patton 2002). The focus groups were particularly useful for providing insights into participants' own "language and concepts" (Tiggemann et al. 2000: 646). This was critical for studying social media use in teens, as it is really important to use the appropriate language with them. I needed to know what a "duck face selfie" or "pro pic" was in order to interview them. I was able to work these terms out when listening to them in the focus group so that I could tailor the interview questions to their language and ideas.
6 In developing the image content analysis, I relied heavily on work in visual sociology guided by Radley and Bell (2007), Bell (2010), and Harper (2012). They advocate the

sociological examination of visual images as an extension of one's narrative, as they tell the viewer who the person is; thus, we study the image as a mechanism for understanding the individual (Radley and Bell 2007; Bell 2010). If images play this role in our lives, it is logical to assume that adolescents use their Facebook to show their "own experiences". I used this rationale for developing codes that emphasized the story of the self. For the more general context analysis such as pose and tone as well as the gender coding, I utilized Goffman's (1979) *Gender Advertisements* as a framework.

Because there is little work done on teens' image making in the field of visual sociology from which to draw upon, I also utilized the "Visual Art Coding Schema" developed by Project Zero (2012) at Harvard to code student photography from high school literary magazines. Although my participants were not working as photographers for the most part, this framework was helpful in thinking about how to describe and evaluate adolescents' photographs.

7 Going into this phase of the research, I was concerned that participants may alter their behavior on Facebook knowing that I was observing them. Perhaps they would take down images that they didn't want me to see or opt not to post certain things. While there can be no way of confirming that this didn't alter their behavior to some degree, I did look at their earlier posts just to confirm that there wasn't a huge difference. As I will highlight later in the book, the powerful norm of presenting the authentic self on social media made it highly unlikely that they could alter their performance in any significant way. However, it is impossible to know for certain whether participants made choices to post or not based on the fact that I was watching.

8 Before I began coding I read through my interviews in their entirety to capture the overall arc of the narrative. The codebook for the interview data was fairly detailed because, although I utilized a grounded theory approach initially, at this point in the analysis I had already developed the salient themes through the focus group analysis and image observation. As a result, I was able to use "focused coding" (Charmaz 2006) on the interview data.

References

Becker, Howard S. 2003. "New Directions in the Sociology of Art" http://home.earthlink.net/~hsbecker

Bell, Philip. 2004. "Content Analysis of Visual Images" in *The Handbook of Visual Analysis*, edited by Theo Van Leeuwen and Carey Jewitt. London, UK: Sage Publications.

Bell, Susan E. 2010. "Visual Methods for Collecting and Analysing Data" Pp. 513–535 in *The Sage Handbook of Qualitative Methods in Health Research*, edited by Ivy Lynn Bourgeault, Raymond DeVries, and Robert Dingwall. London, UK: Sage Publications.

Blair-Loy, Mary. 2001. "Cultural Constructions of Family Schemas: The Case of Women Finance Executives" *Gender and Society* 15: 687–709.

boyd, danah. 2007. "Why Youth (Heart) Social Network Sites: The Role of Networked Publics in Teenage Social Life" in *MacArthur Foundation Series on Digital Learning—Youth, Identity, and Digital Media Volume*, edited by David Buckingham. Cambridge, MA: MIT Press.

———. 2013. "How "Context Collapse" Was Coined: My Recollection" www.zephoria.org/thoughts/archives/2013/12/08/coining-context-collapse.html

———. 2014. *It's Complicated: The Social Lives of Networked Teens*. New Haven, CT: Yale University Press.

Brubaker, Rogers and Frederick Cooper. 2000. "Beyond 'Identity'" *Theory and Society* 29: 1–47.

Charmaz, Kathy. 2006. *Constructing Grounded Theory: A Practical Guide Through Qualitative Analysis*. Thousand Oaks, CA: Sage Publications.

Collins, Randall. 2000. "Situational Stratification: A Micro-Macro Theory of Inequality" *Sociological Theory* 18: 17–43.

Dahl, Ronald E. 2004. "Adolescent Brain Development: A Period of Vulnerabilities and Opportunities" *Academy of Sciences Keynote Address* 102: 1–22.

Davis, Jenny. 2014. "Triangulating the Self: Identity Processes in a Connected Era" *Symbolic Interaction* 37: 500–523.

Davis, Jenny and Nathan Jurgenson. 2011. "Prosuming Identity Online" in *Cyborgology*, edited by Nathan Jurgenson and P.J. Rey. http://thesocietypages.org/cyborgology/

DiMaggio, Paul. 1997. "Culture and Cognition" *Annual Review of Sociology* 23: 263–287.

Edwards, Jim. October 2013. "Facebook Is No Longer the Most Popular Social Network for Teens" *Business Insider*. www.businessinsider.com/facebook-and-teen-user-trends-2013-10

Elder, Glenn H. Jr. August 1975. "Age Differentiation and the Life Course" *Annual Review of Sociology* 1: 165–190.

Elkind, David. 1967. "Egocentrism in Adolescence" *Child Development* 38: 1025–1034.

Erikson, Erik H. 1980. *Identity and the Life Cycle*. New York: W.W. Norton & Company.

Ewing, Katherine P. 1990. "The Illusion of Wholeness: Culture, Self, and the Experience of Inconsistency" *Ethos* 18: 251–278.

Falconer, Ian. 2000. *Olivia*. New York, NY: Simon and Schuster's Children's Publishing Division.

Fine, Gary A. 2004. "Adolescence as Cultural Toolkit: High School Debate and the Repertoires of Childhood and Adulthood" *The Sociological Quarterly* 45: 1–20.

Giddens, Anthony. 1991. *Modernity and Self-Identity: Self and Society in the Late Modern Age*. Stanford, CA: Stanford University Press.

Goffman, Erving. 1959. *The Presentation of Self in Everyday Life*. New York, NY: Anchor Books, Doubleday.

———. 1979. *Gender Advertisements*. New York, NY: Harper and Row Publishers

Harper, Douglas. 2012. *Visual Sociology*. New York, NY: Routledge.

Harrison, Abigail. 2005. "Adolescents Through the Life-Course: Social Context and Determinants of Young People's Sexual Risk in Rural KwaZulu/Natal, South Africa" Working Paper Brown University.

Hine, Christine M. 2000. *Virtual Ethnography*. London, UK: Sage Publications.

Hogan, Bernie. 2010. "The Presentation of Self in the Age of Social Media: Distinguishing Performances and Exhibitions Online" *Bulletin of Science, Technology, and Society* 30: 377–386.

Jacobs, Mark D. and Lyn Spillman. 2005. "Cultural Sociology at the Crossroads of the Discipline" *Poetics* 33: 1–14.

Jurgenson, Nathan and P.J. Rey. 2012. "The Fan Dance: How Privacy Thrives in an Age of Cyber-Publicity" in *Unlike Us Reader: Social Media Monopolies and Their Alternatives*, edited by Geert Lovink and Miriam Rasch. Amsterdam: Institute of Network Cultures.

Katz, James E. and Elizabeth Thomas Crocker. 2015. "Selfies and Photo Messaging as Visual Conversation: Reports From the United States, United Kingdom and China" *International Journal of Communication* 9 (12): 1861–1872.

Lamont, Michele. 2000. *The Dignity of Working Men: Morality and the Boundaries of Race, Class, and Immigration*. New York, NY: The Russell Sage Foundation.

Lamont, Michele and Laurent Thevenot. 2000. "Introduction: Toward a Renewed Comparative Cultural Sociology" in *Rethinking Comparative Cultural Sociology*, edited by Michele Lamont and Laurent Thevenot. Cambridge, UK: Cambridge University Press.

Mendelson, Andrew L. and Zizi Papacharissi. 2010. "Look at Us: Collective Narcissism in College Students Facebook Photo Galleries" in *The Networked Self: Identity, Community and Culture on Social Network Sites*, edited by Zizi Papacharissi. New York, NY: Routledge.

Merton, Robert K. 1957. *Social Theory and Social Structure*. Glencoe, IL: Free Press.

Paget, Marianne A. 1983. "Experience and Knowledge" *Human Studies* 6: 67–90.

Papacharissi, Zizi. (2009). "The Virtual Geographies of Social Networks: A Comparative Analysis of Facebook, LinkedIn, and ASmallWorld." *New Media & Society* 11 (1–2), 199–220.

Pascoe, C.J. 2010. "Intimacy" in *Hanging Out, Messing Around, and Geeking Out*, edited by Mizuko Ito. Cambridge, MA: MIT Press.

Patton, Michael Q. (2002). *Qualitative Research and Evaluation Methods*. Third Edition. Thousand Oaks, CA: Sage Publications.

Postill, John and Sarah Pink. 2012. "Social Media Ethnography: The Digital Researcher a Messy Web" *Media International Australia* 145: 123–134.

Project Zero "Visual Art Coding Scheme" shared by Carrie James in 2012.

Radley, Alan and Susan Elizabeth Bell. 2007. "Artworks, Collective Experience and Claims for Social Justice: The Case of Women Living With Breast Cancer" *Sociology of Health and Illness* 29: 366–390.

Robinson, Laura. 2007. "The Cyberself: The Self-ing Project Goes Online, Symbolic Interaction in the Digital Age" *New Media Society* 9: 93–110.

Robinson, Laura, Sheila R. Cotten, Hiroshi Obo, Anabel Quaan-Hasse, Gustavo Mesch, Wenhong Chen, Jeremy Schulz, Timothy M. Hale, and Michael J. Stern. 2015. "Digital Inequalities and Why They Matter" *Information, Communication & Society* 18 (5): 569–582.

Sales, Nancy Jo. 2016. *American Girls: Social Media and the Secret Lives of Teenagers*. New York, NY: Alfred A. Knopf.

Sims, Christo. October 22, 2007. "Composed Conversations: Teenage Practices of Flirting With New Media" Society for the Social Studies of Science Conference. Montreal, Canada.

Smith, Christian and Melinda L. Denton. 2005. *Soul Searching: The Religious and Spiritual Lives of American Teenagers*. Oxford, UK: Oxford University Press.

Somers, Margaret R. 1994. "The Narrative Constitution of Identity: A Relational and Network Approach" *Theory and Society* 23: 605–649.

Thorlindsson, Thorolfur and Jon G. Bernburg. 2006. "Peer Groups and Substance Use: Examining the Direct and Interactive Effect of Leisure Activity" *Adolescence* 41: 321–339.

Tiggemann, Marika, Maria Gardiner, and Amy Slater. 2000. "'I Would Rather Be a Size 10 Than Get Straight A's': A Focus Group Study of Adolescent Girls' Wish to Be Thinner" *Journal of Adolescence* 23: 645–659.

Tufecki, Zeynep. 2008. "Can You See Me Now? Audience and Disclosure Regulation in Online Social Networking Sites" *Bulletin of Science, Technology and Society* 28: 20–36.

Turkle, Sherry. 2011. *Alone Together: Why We Expect More From Technology and Less From Each Other*. New York, NY: Basic Books.

Vartarian, Lessa Rae. 2000. "Revisiting the Imaginary Audience and Personal Fable Constructs of Adolescent Egocentrism: A Conceptual Review" *Adolescence* 35: 639–661.

Walther, Joseph B., Brandon Van Der Heide, Sang-Yeon Kim, David Westerman, and Stephanie Tom Tong. 2008. "The Role of Friends' Appearance and Behavior on Evaluations of Individuals on Facebook: Are We Known by the Company We Keep? *Human Communication Research* 34 (1): 28–49.

Wilkins, Amy C. 2008. *Wannabes, Goths, and Christians: The Boundaries of Sex, Style, and Status*. Chicago, IL: University of Chicago Press.

Zarghooni, Sasan. Autumn 2007. "A Study of Self-Presentation in Light of Facebook" Institute of Psychology, University of Oslo.

Zhao, Shanyang, Sherri Grasmuck, and Jason Martin. 2008. "Identity Construction on Facebook: Digital Empowerment in Anchored Relationships" *Computers in Human Behavior* 24: 1816–1836.

1 Creating the visual narrative
"It's their highlight reel that they're showing you"

A prom picture of a well-dressed couple posing together. A picture of an unsmiling girl in a bikini on the beach, staring into the camera. A photo of a boy playing sports, his face obscured by his equipment. A smiling close-up picture of a teen on a trip. A selfie of a girl sitting on her boyfriend's lap. A close-up of a girl making a goofy face on the train. These were some of the profile pictures I examined over the course of my social media observations. These images were important, because they made a social media first impression. And naturally, we want our first impressions to reflect our best selves. As one twelfth-grade boy described it, "I always think of it as like someone else's like, it's their highlight reel [of their life], that they're showing you."

On any app or site that relies on visual communication the architecture will dictate the different components that make up the "highlights reel," but most sites rely on a "profile picture" or first picture that comes to represent the first impression. The key thing is that all of these sites or apps have some type of introduction (first picture, caption, biography, etc.) that forms our first impression to the audiences. On Facebook, a teen's "highlights reel" is made up of three components: profile and cover photos, related but less significant timeline images and photo albums, and the numbers game (i.e., the number of friends you have and the number of likes you receive for your images). The teens I interviewed told me they devote the most time and care to their profile and cover photos. Timeline pictures serve to "back up" the first impression, thus assuring that sought-after authenticity. The images and metrics that other teens can see instantly essentially come to signify a teen's social media front stage. Just as our offline front stage is our best performance, which we accomplish via the management of the impressions we give and give off (Goffman 1959), the same is true of our social media front stage as well. And again, this work has multiple audiences and participants: the social media friends who can generate likes and other content, and who also assess the content; and the poster, who assesses the responses he or she receives.

In this chapter, I present some of the images and excerpts from my interviews to show how the "highlights reel" self that teens construct on social media invokes Goffman's (1959) concept of impression management. The teens I interviewed said that their focus is on creating the performance that will highlight the "best" parts of their personal fable. Again, no image can tell the full story, but the key point of the front stage presentation is to make sure that what gets seen first are the images that the teen believes to represent some of his or her greatest moments. The idea that the images teens select are a "highlights reel" of their stories is compelling and links well to Goffman's notion of the front stage performance. Importantly, this does not feel like inauthentic work, nor is it perceived as generic; Goffman's concept acknowledges both the specificity and generalizability of the performance.

Later in the book, I argue that this surface self-presentation is meaningful, but the image typologies presented in this chapter may not always appear to be meaningful to the reader. Particularly if the reader is over the age of 25! Or rather, the images are meaningful to us, but mainly because they seem to emphasize our worst fears about teenage life or the most cliché aspects of adolescence—the social meanness, the focus on appearance, risk taking, and overt sexuality. This was certainly my position when I began this project. These images seemed so trite and banal that initially I could not understand the draw to post them on social media. And so similar! Why do they all need to recreate the same images over and over again on social media? It is this surface self-presentation, full of bikini pictures, jock pictures, and party pictures, that garners the most attention in the popular press. But these images *are* important, surprisingly so, even if, at first glance, they do not seem all that positive. Later in the book, I will focus on the effects of these images and teens' motivations for posting them, but for now, I want to show the typical "highlights reel" images, as most of them said that the work to create and curate the first impression takes a great deal of their time and effort. As a reminder, these images represent new content the teen chooses to create, and as such, these are the images that are produced "alone in my room in my pajamas," giving these teens time to think through their image selection. And, too, these are the images that they most want their audiences to see; we need to understand what they want to convey if we hope to understand what meanings they make and take from their presentation work on social media.

The online personal fable

Profile pictures are the cornerstone images of teens' highlights reels. They all told me that their Facebook profile picture was the most important picture and was the one for which they expected to receive the most likes. Indeed, all the girls told me that it is just an expectation that "all your friends will like your profile picture." These important images are certainly an opportunity to show one's best self; however, interestingly, they very rarely operate outside of the boundaries of the personal fable—although, as mentioned in the introduction, in some images it is harder to see or infer the fable than in others. Teens have to balance their highlights reel with their fable. For most of the teens in the study, this is not as hard as it may sound. For a few notable outliers who will be discussed later, this can be a very difficult balance to strike.

The highlights reel of the fable can be either very obvious or more subtle. It can be as direct as a boy who thinks of himself as a good athlete using a sports image as his profile picture, or a girl who thinks of herself as a good friend choosing an image that shows her with a good friend. Images can also be more subtle. A boy might highlight his nonconformity, for example, by posting unflattering images. (I want to point out here that these examples may appear to be reductive of gender stereotypes, but as I illustrate in Chapter 3, these teens are vigilant about upholding traditional norms around masculinity and femininity. Thus while my examples may seem to verge on the cliché, they are what I observed in the data.) When images can really speak to an important part of a teen's fable, particularly qualities that might be harder to articulate than athleticism or social prowess, participants spoke about their images in ways that indicated that they represent more than simply a flattering surface picture of them. Gebre, an 18-year-old male participant, posted a picture of himself that shows him anxiously waiting to hear whether or not he was accepted to an elite university (see Figure 1.1).

Although the image was taken while he was waiting to hear from the school, he waited until after he learned of his acceptance to post it. The image received 117 likes, which for the boys in this study was an incredibly high number (to put this in perspective, the average for males during the observation period was about five likes). Gebre captioned this picture: "Yesterday . . . Waiting to hear back from [elite school] . . . Its not like I was nervous or anything." This self-reflective caption shows that Gebre is willing to share his emotions and vulnerabilities, indicating that he was nervous and clearly appeared very stressed. But the image also serves to highlight his success. It is especially telling that he waited to post the image until after he was accepted; perhaps it is easier to be vulnerable after the outcome is guaranteed. In talking to Gebre, though, it was clear that this obvious

Figure 1.1   Gebre Waiting to Hear About College Admissions

"highlight reel" moment showcasing his college acceptance revealed more to his peers about him than just his success. His discussion of the image is illustrative of the power of the highlights reel and the personal fable coming together. When I asked Gebre to tell me about this picture, he said:

> I had a status before I posted that, that was talking about like, 'cause I wasn't born here, I was born in Ethiopia . . . And like it's something that's like very rare for somebody to be able to go and do that [getting into an elite college]. And like my socioeconomic class is like one of the lowest in like the school. And so like it's difficult for a person like me to get into a school like this . . . And I posted this picture because it represented like the feeling. Yeah 'cause pictures speak a lot of words.

In this brief excerpt from our dialogue, Gebre highlights some important aspects of his fable, notably the obstacles he has faced to earn admission to this school: he is an immigrant and is, compared to his peers at school, of a lower socioeconomic class. During the interview, Gebre referred often to the notion of achievement in the face of challenge. Focusing solely on the image's highlights reel interpretation would lead us to see this as a picture signaling, "I got into a great school." While it does do this, Gebre made it clear that the image also tells the "I got into a great school in spite of many obstacles" component of his fable. And perhaps most pointedly, it clarifies that he's faced many obstacles his classmates have not. As he said, "Pictures speak a lot of words," and for him this image represented the feeling of his inner narrative and is therefore meaningful for him.

Supporting the notions of adolescent development and the personal fable, this narrative highlights Gebre's uniqueness (Elkind 1967). What is interesting about the image is that while the highlights reel function is obvious to all, its connection to his fable is not immediately clear to the broader audience. While the image and caption suggest that he is nervous about being accepted, one would have to know him fairly well to understand the link to his fable about how hard he's worked, as a child of immigrants who did not grow up with money, to get here. As he states, "It takes a lot of work and I worked really hard for it." This introduces another nuance of the highlights reel: the links to the personal fable and its significance need only be understood by the poster. What matters in this case is that Gebre *feels* this connection, even if it is not readily understood by his peers.

Thinking of teens' Facebook profiles in this way challenges the popularly held notion that adolescents post social media content with very little thought for what it may mean or the consequences. Though I did come across photos that were posted with very little forethought, most of these were reported to be posted under the influence of alcohol and none were selected as profile pictures. And, as I will argue in the following chapter, while the initial posting may have been rash, the choice to keep these pictures, which can easily be removed or untagged, is a highly thought-out and strategic choice to signal certain behaviors, friendships, or even aspects of the emerging self.

When we engage in the front stage performance, we do not present all sides of ourselves. Just as a physical photo album contains only our best pictures—our most flattering images and images of our best experiences—so, too, social media collects the images that, as a twelfth-grade boy said, "document us being awesome." They may be awesome moments, but they reflect an ideal reality. The key point is that they feel authentic. One twelfth-grade girl referred to her Facebook profile as an accurate portrayal of herself with "maybe more flattering pictures." While they have different definitions of what makes them awesome, teens select images with the goal of presenting the best versions of themselves.

It may go without saying, then, that part of impression management and face-saving (Goffman 1955, 1959) means teens avoid calling attention to their fears and failures. This was certainly true of the images I observed in the study.

In a few cases, some of the boys would share an academic challenge, but it was reframed as a joke.[1] One boy, for instance, posted a picture showing his low grade on a chemistry test and crowned himself "Jeff Silver Chem God" in a status update, which was well received by his male peers. (Based on the social media gender norms I observed that allow for high levels of male idiocy among participants, it is not clear that this low grade would constitute a failure for him; or rather, an academic failure may be acceptable socially.)

While they work hard to acquire certain images, some participants reported that they are just as strategic about what they choose to leave off social media as they are about what to post. Adolescents do not post every photo they take, even if it may seem that way given the sheer quantity of their images on social media, nor do they present every facet of their personal fable on Facebook. One ninth-grade girl said,

> Cause I'm, I'm kind of a nerd, um, I, I try to post like achievements. Um, but, I mean there's also like, oh I don't want to post this because I don't want to be like, "Look at me. I got like this [award] . . ." Like I got an award in Spanish but I didn't post it because I didn't want people to be, like, "Oh god it's her again."

Although she acknowledges that her fable is that she is "kind of a nerd," she does not want this presentation to dominate her social media images, or at least not too often. While she expresses an initial desire to post the image, she makes the decision to hold back, suggesting controlled and thoughtful impression management work.

Emphasis on appearance and the front stage

As indicated by the previous example, the first impression management work teens have to do on Facebook is to decide what to post (Kramer and Winter 2008). When I asked them about the impression they were trying to create with their images on Facebook, all teens had a clear answer and rationale for the images they selected. Image choices are rarely arbitrary or unimportant. Tom, an articulate twelfth-grade boy with an interest in politics, said that he often thinks of the image he presents on social media because

> I'm always worried like, I've always liked politics. And I've always been worried about what they're gonna say about our Facebooks and Twitters later . . . so I guess I'm always kind of worried about like the image I give off. That's why I tend not to use Facebook liberally; um, I usually interact with other people's things instead of posting my own.

The fear about how his image may be interpreted in the future has led Tom to play a more passive role on Facebook, responding to others' pictures and comments rather than posting a large amount of his own original content.

Others negotiate their impression management "highlights reel" on Facebook by actively engaging in the creation and development of social media content. In particular, they pay close attention to ensuring they have images that signal their appearance and social belonging, both of which can be managed, within reason, through image selection. While everyone wants to look good on social media, for my participants what constitutes flattering imagery on social media is gendered. Although gender will be discussed more fully in Chapter 3, it is important to note here, as the gendered norms around what constitutes a "flattering" image are an integral component of the cultivation of the highlights reel. Girls will organize photo shoots to craft images and ensure that they look pretty, or improve images using photo-editing apps. Because it is socially acceptable for girls to care about appearance, they can invest a bit more time in their labor to produce flattering images. Every participant in the study, including the boys, could articulate the point of the photo shoot, and while some of the girls were a bit embarrassed to talk about their own photo shoot images, they did feel that it was normal for girls to have a photo shoot image as a profile picture.

Boys, who uniformly reported that it is not masculine behavior to take or pose for pictures, still want to look like their best selves in their images. With the exception of two boys, Matt and Noah, all of the other boys indicated that it is important to them to look good in their profile pictures.[2]

For boys, appearance is important, but the challenge for them in this realm is that it is deemed feminine to take pictures and to appear to care a lot about your appearance. As such, many said that they have to rely on others to take pictures. This may explain why boys have fewer images, and while it certainly affects their ability to control their appearance, it is clear in talking to them that despite fewer images, they think about it a lot, even if they cannot ensure their success.

When I asked Jake how boys negotiate this balance between masculine norms and wanting to get a good picture, he said, "Poorly, we do it poorly." Some boys elaborated, talking about how they rely on their parents to take a great athletic shot, which gets around having to take the picture and ensures you appear athletic and manly in your images. Others talked about cropping themselves out of a group picture if they look good in it. Peter and Gebre both explained how to subtly set up a male version of a photo shoot in a group setting without making it obvious you want a picture. For Gebre, getting a flattering profile picture clearly requires a great deal of strategizing and effort. It's important for him to appear to have put in very little effort. As he said, "You have to be like, 'I look good without even trying to look good.' Like, 'I'm just going on with my business but I'm looking good.'" While the girls' photo shoots generate images intended to be flattering, the boys have to appear more circumspect, at least in the offline creation of the image.

Social belonging and the front stage

Because of the collaborative nature of the social media platform (Hogan 2010; Davis 2014), a key component of impression management is to showcase social belonging. Again, first impressions are powerful: these teens unanimously said they can assess "popularity" or social position based on image content (in particular who is in the image), the number of likes users receive, and the number of friends they have. In all four of the focus groups, teens reported that they could comfortably assess a person's social position just by knowing the number of likes he or she received on an image, especially if the number is low. As one twelfth-grade girl remarked, "I've noticed other people who are like less cool . . . less people would like [the image] and no one would really comment on it." She suggests that the "less cool" kids in her class have a different amount of social interaction on social media, and therefore, she felt confident using likes as a measure to assess people.

Image subject matter is also indicative of social belonging, as teens who are socially connected can post images that show more kids (and similarly will be tagged in more pictures), particularly popular high-status kids, and at more "cool events," as the teens described them to me. One twelfth-grade girl said, "It's more like they might post, I mean it depends on the person but they might post . . . like a big group of girls together," implying that the sheer quantity of people in a picture can signal social position. This component of social status has been well documented, but it is important to mention here because these adolescents are fully aware that social media images usually reveal social belonging; however, it is also important to note that none of the participants believe that social media can influence one's position in the social hierarchy. Social capital, according to them, is not manufactured on social media. The work they do with their images is not done to gain status, but rather to create a visual representation of their social belonging—although to be sure, a major social transgression on social media could have implications in offline social relationships.

The balance between authenticity and the highlights reel

Of course, the highlights reel cannot veer too far from a teen's constructed authentic self. As such, a component of the work they do is to balance the highlights with what they deem to be the "real me." And again, our work here is not to determine whether they are in fact being authentic, but rather to understand what feels authentic to them. In the interview Chris, a confident and athletic twelfth-grade boy, described his Facebook as "pretty realistic" and felt that the guy you meet in person would match "the guy on Facebook." Most of Chris' images are action shots of him playing sports. In one such picture, which shows Chris in his lacrosse uniform on the field, he captioned, "2 sports in the spring?" Chris' picture is authentic because he actually does play the two sports, lacrosse and golf, but it is also clearly a highlights reel image as it is selected and captioned to send important signals about his athleticism, a trait coveted by the teenage boys in this study. While Chris does not do these activities so he can post on Facebook, his choice to post with this caption shows how authenticity and the highlights reel can work together to showcase the "best" self.

Similarly, Izzy, a smiley earnest ninth-grade girl with a huge mass of thick brown curls, spoke at length about the strategy and work involved in coordinating her profile-picture photo shoots with friends, which are created expressly to show the highlights reel. In this study only girls participated in photo shoots, but all the participants were aware of them and felt that they could assess easily whether the image they were looking at came from a photo shoot. Photo shoots typically involve female friends getting together with the express purpose of producing images for social media. This process will be detailed in Chapter 3, but it is important to note here that the photo shoot images involve a great deal of coordination and time to achieve the end result of a flattering picture of a girl or group of girls to show on social media. This is the highlights reel in all its glory: posing, primping, and manufacturing images to present the best version of the self. Yet, interestingly, when I asked many of the girls about their photo shoot images, they were quick to argue that while the images are manufactured, they are also authentic. When I asked Izzy about her photo shoot images, she said, "But I take [pictures] of my friends all the time. . . . Like I'm not trying to make it look cool or anything, I'm just taking a picture." Girls saw these photo shoots as fun times with friends, not as stressful experiences to get an image. In some ways, it can be viewed as a form of bonding. Although at another point in the interview Izzy describes the "arty" photo shoots, here Izzy is quick to downplay her strategies and effort to create her Facebook presence. In this moment, she focuses on the natural and everyday aspect of her pictures, thus highlighting the authentic nature of the image. And again, the point is not to judge the authenticity of her images, but rather to note that Izzy believes it is natural for girls to take flattering images of their friends.

Talk about the "real me" and the everyday nature of the images is a form of Goffman's face-saving (1955); it is far less risky to say, "This is just what I look like" or "I'm just taking pictures" than to admit that you really worked hard to craft a presentation of the self. While face-saving is important to these teens, it is critical to be able to "back it up" offline, as one boy described, meaning that you cannot stray too far from your everyday presentation. A flattering picture is acceptable, but something that goes beyond that, to the point where you no longer look like yourself, is not. These findings offer a counterbalance to the research done by Turkle (2011), in which she argues that teens often present very different or altered versions of the self on social media. The boys in particular felt that it was very important to be authentic and spoke about the negative reactions some boys receive when their images do not represent an authentic presentation for that person. As Myles put it, "The thing at [my school] is if you post like something [inauthentic] . . . people will call you out on it. . . . And if like, let's say it's like, disguising yourself . . . six guys will rip on you . . . for like a [class] period." Although I learned about this experience mostly from boys telling me about things they observed happening to others versus things they experienced themselves, I did have one boy in the study who struggled with this and was ridiculed for his social media images. For example, he posted many basketball pictures, which could give the impression that he was very good, a fact that was not necessarily the case. He was known to a few boys in the study, who described him as an example of someone who lost social status because he was not authentic on social media; Myles, who knows the boy but is not close friends with him, mentioned that he observed that "people posted like really mean things to him when he was young." In this case there were negative social repercussions for presenting images that were deemed inauthentic by his peers. This boy discussed this experience in his interview, and his story will be presented in greater depth in Chapter 4, but he made it clear that this experience also had a negative psychosocial impact on him, affecting his self-esteem and friendships. Boys call each other on their inaccuracies and exaggerations, and while girls may not do the same verbally, they did report that they judge inauthentic people as "trying too hard" or "fake." And yet, in the case of the boy's mistake outlined above, I cannot help but wonder if his images were just misread by his peers? What if he just loved to play basketball and wanted to show that it was important to him in spite of the fact that he is not a star player? Can't the JV kids show their images too? When I pushed back in cases like this, participants would tell me that you "just know" or "well you know what the person is like so you can tell." In essence, they were judging the image based on what they know about the person—if you boast in an inauthentic way in person, they can read the image as trying to pose as a star player; if you don't, it could be read as an image that just shows your love of basketball. This is a clear example of why it is not possible to separate the online from the offline. But ultimately, it is also evidence that it is a challenge to navigate the balance between showing an authentic highlights and overdoing the reel self on Facebook.

Setting the stage: the all-important profile picture

All the teens I interviewed told me that profile pictures matter most, as these images help to create their first impression. Impression work is risky in general, but it is particularly so when that impression is made visually, and usually to a wide audience; indeed, many participants had 1,000+ Facebook friends. As a result, the teens generally selected very safe and flattering profile pictures that mirrored their friends' images. Thus while the profile picture was important to them, it was probably the least indicative of the inner personal fable. Almost all of the profile pictures I observed, irrespective of the age or gender of the poster, fell into two categories of the surface self: some emphasized appearance and others showcased friendships and social belonging. This suggests that what is important to convey in a first impression is either the physical self or the social self. Family, extracurricular activities, and anything with a serious tone (such as politics or academics) were absent from profile pictures. The only exception to this was that for a brief time during the observation period two of the girls changed their profile pictures to red equal signs to indicate their support for marriage equality. This was not the norm, nor did they keep these images for long. Interestingly, several of the boys mocked this type of thing in the interviews, saying that girls only do this to "jump on the bandwagon" of the latest trendy movement, not because they really believe in the cause. In this case, the boys are challenging the authenticity of these girls' profile pictures.[3] And, interestingly, the boys are implying that the girls' use of these images is more about signaling social belonging (i.e., "jumping on the bandwagon" with their friends) rather than signaling their deep belief in a political cause or movement; while certainly the girls do support marriage equality, the boys believe they only change their profile picture to show their support because their friends have done so. Girls in the study were divided; some referred to it as "just going along with what's trendy" while others believed it demonstrated true ideological beliefs.

In general, the girls in the study had virtually identical profile pictures; while none were overtly revealing of the body, all highlighted physical appearance. Indeed, many of the girls said that the whole point of the profile picture is to present a flattering image of the physical self. Cooley (1964) argues that the body becomes important for the self when it holds a "social function or significance." Social media gives the body a significant social function as a key way for teens, particularly girls, to show the "awesome." Although this research cannot speak to the effects on teens of being "on display" (Entwistle and Mears 2012) on social media in a physical way, it is important to note that the physical self is constantly presented, viewed, and evaluated on social media. And positive feedback on appearance is incredibly important to these teens. Figures 1.2 and 1.3 are two girls' profile pictures from the study. The first girl is 16 and the girl in the second image is 18. They do not attend the same school, yet the images are remarkably similar; the pictures are posed and showcase the girls in a traditionally flattering way. In the first picture, we do see a glimpse of a model pose in her bent knee, but it is a fairly standard pose that, along with the arm-on-the-hip pose, has been co-opted by most of the girls in the study. It is important to note that while every girl in the study used the model pose in at least some pictures, girls in general had very similar image typologies (which will be explored in the next two chapters in greater detail), and as such, I think this is more about having a flattering picture and creating content that mirrors their friends' content in order to signal social belonging rather than some desire to appear as a model. Indeed, girls went out of their way to tell me that they were not interested in comparing themselves to celebrities or models. Instead they opt to compare themselves to their peers.

Marie, the twelfth-grade girl pictured in Figure 1.3, who had just uploaded this picture in the days before we met, said that she wanted to change her picture to one from her junior prom because this type of image (i.e., those that show the girls dressed up for an important event) tends to "do well" on social media, by which she means that these images will get a lot of likes. Thus with this image Marie can showcase her appearance, in the image, and social belonging, in the number

Figure 1.2 Carly's Profile Picture

of likes, both of which are important to her. She walked me through her decision
to post this image:

> So then it's like, "Oh all of these are horrible," so I kind of just was looking
> through and. . . 'cause . . . I don't really change my profile picture that often
> so I was kind of thinking I should just change it and so um, I was like, "Why

Figure 1.3 Marie's Profile Picture Taken Before Prom

don't I just do it for prom because everyone else is" . . . And like I'd get the opportunity for a lot of people to like it because a lot of people were like liking pictures so, and [my sister] said she liked that one so I just like decided to do that one and . . . I felt like that was like the best one.

Marie notes that her motivation for changing her image came from the realization that "everyone else is" posting pictures like this and getting a lot of likes, and therefore the image would "do well," to use her language. In posting this image, Marie makes a safe decision; based on her observations of her friends' experiences with similar images, she feels almost like she is guaranteed to get likes from friends, thus creating a successful first impression. Again, we do not see much of the individual in the profile picture; this image tells us little about her beyond the fact that she went to prom, looks pretty in her dress, and got a lot of likes, but that is enough for the profile picture first impression.

While the boys' profile pictures are similar to the girls' in that they are also either generally flattering or focused on friendships, boys do seem to have more freedom in their image selection, which will be discussed further in Chapters 2 and 3. Boys do care about physical appearance, but they have a variety of ways to showcase this and also tend to highlight experiences in their profile pictures more often than girls. For example, one boy used a picture showing a group of friends at a concert as his profile picture, while several others had pictures showing them playing sports. Boys also had fewer close-up shots of the face, a point that bothered many of the girls, who noted that "you can never see what they look like," which they felt should be the point of the profile picture. When I asked boys about this, they said that those types of close-up headshots are "girly" and so they rarely utilized them. In contrast, the girls almost universally opted for traditionally flattering individual profile pictures in which you can clearly see their faces.

But while the images may be different depending on the gender of the poster, in most cases these teens adhered fairly closely to the notion of the "ideal self" generic presentation for profile pictures that follows the social norms. It is important to note, however, that if there is a chance an image may appeal to someone the poster is interested in romantically, he or she might be willing to take a risk and break with the norms. It is in these instances that you see overtly sexualized images or images that run counter to gender norms. In Gebre's picture (Figure 1.4), he clearly cropped out others in order to highlight himself.

This image is more typical of the girls' profile pictures than the boys': it is a close-up of his face, it appears posed, and it is hard to determine where he is or what he is doing. In the interview, he said that the picture was taken on a school trip and that he chose to cut the other people out so that he would be the focal point of the picture. When I asked him how he would evaluate it, he said, "I think girls would like that. I think some guys would be like, 'That's a borderline selfie' . . . But it's like, I don't care." He went on to add that he thought he looked

Figure 1.4 Gebre's "Borderline Selfie" Profile Picture

really good in the image, another reason he was willing to post the picture. Gebre was willing to break some of the gendered rules about boys taking "selfies" when he thought it was an image that would appeal to girls.

In another example, Chris posted a picture from his prom that resembled many of the girls' prom pictures; Chris and his date are in semiformal dress standing together (she in the model pose with her hand on her hip) in front of a fireplace in someone's living room. They stand very close together, arms around each other, and both are smiling. While Chris used this image as his profile picture, he did not post the original picture. The girl in the picture with him posted it and tagged Chris, at which point he chose to take the image and make it his profile picture. When I asked Chris about this picture he noted that he selected it because it was a good picture of him. Similar to Gebre, he highlights appearance as one of the reasons to select this picture for the profile picture; however, he was also quick to point out that he did not take or originally post the picture, attributing its appearance on social media entirely to the girl in the picture. With this picture, Chris is working to balance highlighting appearance while also ensuring his adherence to gender norms about taking and posting pictures.

Similarly, Tom posted a profile picture that was also a close-up of his face, again challenging some of the male norms. However, in his image he is dressed in a coat and tie and appears to be standing before an audience, although the background audience is blurry and therefore it is hard to see where he is and what he is doing. Although he did not title the image, the viewer can assume that it presents an achievement or success of some kind given his dress and audience. I talked to Tom about his choice of a close-up of his face for his profile picture, and he told me it was a picture from his graduation and "everyone likes a guy who's well dressed." While his image and comments may be more focused on appearance, he did not take or coordinate the picture (everyone takes pictures of everyone at graduation), and the image highlights an important event, something that is important to boys. In all three of these cases, boys are trying to present a version of the highlights reel that ensures that they look good; however, Tom and Chris do so in ways that ensure they retain their masculinity by using images that others post to social media. Gebre is willing to take more of a chance because he believes that his image will be appealing to girls.

Backing up the first impression: timeline and album images

Most of the teens' supporting images, images that come from their timelines and photo albums, also focus on documenting the self and one's social belonging, although in these images we start to see more diversity in experiences and interests represented and image selection. Some of the most common image typologies that can be seen in the supporting images are those that represent friendship. The images that document friendships are important because social belonging is important for adolescents' conception of the self. Every teen I talked to mentioned the importance of showcasing friendships on social media. Clearly, Zhao et al.'s

(2008) notion of "know me by my friends" is a critical component of social media for these adolescents. Irrespective of gender, when peers are visible, the majority are same-sex peers.

Girls' pictures with their friends fall into two archetypes. The first are extremely flattering, stylized shots of girls posed close together (often touching) and looking at the camera in ways that communicate to the viewer, "Look at us, we are good friends, happy, and so attractive." This first type of image is fairly standard. In one example, Sara posted a picture of her and a "close friend" at their high school graduation. They are both looking at the camera, smiling, and their heads are touching. Although the image is only taken from the shoulders up, based on their body angles, it looks as though they might have been hugging. This image signals that these girls are attractive, good friends, and at a happy event. This type of image reminds me of the pictures of friends I saved in photo albums in the pre-social media era.

The second kind of image depicting friendships are the goofy/silly shots that send a slightly different message; these signal "Look at us, we are so hilarious." Both types of images of friends highlight that the peer group is fun, and even the silly shots are still flattering images, at least in terms of highlighting positive social experiences if not physically flattering. Figure 1.5, posted by a twelfth-grade girl, captures a fun moment with a friend before class. Although this picture is not flattering in the traditional way that the more posed images used for profile

Figure 1.5 Lucy and a Friend Posed Before Class

pictures are, it still is a bit evocative in the presentation of the body, particularly in the stance of the girl on the left. Lucy, the girl on the right, was tagged in the picture and it received four likes. The tone is humorous and they are posed close together, indicating a fun, close friendship, and perhaps by extension suggesting that they themselves are fun and funny. Girls' "fun" pictures often retained a sexual component, and I sometimes found myself double coding their images as playful and sexy/flirtatious in my analysis of the images.

In another example of this, Cassie included several pictures that the teens referred to as a "bathroom mirror selfie."[4] I saw bathroom mirror selfies taken of just one individual or sometimes of groups of girls. In Cassie's selfies from this series (several were posted with slightly different poses), she and her friends are posed in their school bathroom. In one image she and a friend are posing with one hand on hip, hip jutted forward, and head tilted to the side. One girl's face is hidden by the camera (she is the photographer) while the other girl is making a silly face. Like Lucy's image described above, this bathroom mirror selfie is simultaneously silly and flirtatious. This dichotomy, evident more often in girls' images than boys', will be explored further in Chapter 3.

Boys' pictures with peers fall into three slightly different categories: 1) goofy pictures where everyone looks like they could care less about their appearance, 2) pictures with friends at cool events, such as sporting events, school trips, and parties, and 3) pictures with girls. These typologies will be explored more in Chapter 3, but a few brief illustrations will be helpful here. An example of how boys' silly friend pictures differ from girls' pictures can be seen via Noah, the twelfth-grade boy who posted Figure 1.6.

Figure 1.6 Noah's Profile Picture With Friends

Like Lucy's image, the tone here is silly and playful; however, unlike Lucy's, there is no emphasis on the physical appearance or the body. Indeed, it is hard to see what the boys look like given the angles and the fact that their faces are cropped. While this may on the surface seem like a bad picture, and it certainly does not give us much information about the context, it is clear that they are relaxed and having fun together, thereby indicating something positive about their friendships. This important signal gives it value on social media.

Pictures at "cool events" often entail sporting events, travel, and, interestingly, time in the car (often traveling to and from fun events). One boy posted a picture of his friends at a professional sporting event, some showed their attendance at key school events (covered in face paint at Homecoming weekend and the like), and many posted images from trips that they had taken (generally the only time family appeared in their images). I did find it interesting that several of the boys posted pictures of their time on buses or in cars as they traveled to and from different events. These were often to athletic events (which tend to be all male) or "road trips" (mixed gender). These images signal that the boys are capable, both financially and socially, to attend these events. Girls have these images, too, highlighting attendance at a fun event, and indeed it is often these images that were a great source of stress and distress among the girls, who reported that it is very hard to see pictures of groups of their friends on social media at some fun event only to realize that they were not included.

In the focus groups and interviews, the boys placed a lot of emphasis on the importance of having pictures with the opposite sex. I was told by virtually every boy that having pictures with girls, preferably "hot girls," on your social media feed is a way to signal your social worth to both boys and girls. Kenny, a twelfth-grade boy, said that they will "pick those pictures of you with attractive girls" and make sure those are on their social media. Matt said he feels like a "big part of like. . . social media in general" is to present the self to girls. Because he is in a relationship, Matt feels that he does not have to look great in pictures to impress girls, unlike many of his unattached friends. Although in spite of this comment, Matt has his own versions of a "hot girl" picture; Matt has many pictures in his Facebook feed of his girlfriend. Often the images were originally posted by his girlfriend, who tagged him in the image. These images are interesting because in the majority of them Matt's face is obscured by hers. This is either because he is kissing her cheek (and the camera is facing her head on) or because of the lighting. In one picture the two are kissing in front of a window on a sunny day and the lighting makes it impossible to see either of their faces beyond the silhouette. I think this version of the "hot girl" picture is interesting as he highlights her appearance and also the intimacy between them through their body language and kiss. Interestingly, in these images he is not showing his appearance but rather focusing on hers. In the interview Matt indicated that showing a picture of a "hot girl" had greater implications for his highlights reel than showing a flattering picture of the self.

Max, another twelfth-grade boy, who does not have a girlfriend, had several great exemplars of the pictures with "hot girls." In one picture, he is flanked by three girls who appear, based on their poses and the abundance of Solo cups, to be intoxicated. The girls' clothes are also fairly revealing, and Max, with a big smile on his face, has his arm around the two closest to him. He was tagged in this picture, and it was captioned "PIMP." It received five likes, four from boys. When I asked Max about this picture, he said that it was taken on a spring sports training trip with his team. He said he was humoring older boys on his team by taking a picture with these girls, who were "completely plastered," by his account. He said he knew that the image was going to end up on social media when it was taken and was fine with that because he felt the photo sent the message that he was a "flaming success" with the ladies. He said this with humor, mocking himself and the image, but he had no intentions of taking down the picture. Perhaps this is Max's hoped-for reality.

Documenting the self

Timeline and album images that document the self are also more diverse than profile pictures and therefore more difficult to place into easy typologies. When the self does get highlighted in these images, it can often be in the context of travel or activities such as arts, theater, and sports. Several teens showed examples of service work they had done, with one posing with some young children he mentored on a summer service trip and another showing an image of himself posing with some of the elderly adults he worked with at a nursing home.

Some teens do use timeline or album pictures to overemphasize the physical self, with girls selecting sexualized images like the close-up that Kate posted (Figure 1.7), in which her lips are parted and she is running her hands through

Figure 1.7 Kate's Timeline Picture

her hair. The comments these types of images receive, typically from same-sex friends, usually refer to appearance. Kate received a comment on this picture from a girl that just said "sex."

The most prevalent type of body conscious images that girls posted in the observation period were bikini pictures, and this is especially interesting given that very few of the girls were part of the study during summer months, when it would typically be bathing suit season in the Northeast. The bikini pictures can run the gamut from girls posed on the beach, smiling, to more provocative images, sometimes entirely unconnected to a beach/pool context. And girls often have both types of bikini pictures in their feed. Carly posted an image of herself in a bikini on the beach wearing sunglasses and smiling. She cropped someone out of the picture, as there is an arm around her waist, but with her editing she has made herself the clear focus of the image. She received 16 likes and two comments about how "sexy" and "pretty" she looked. However, she posted another picture that has a different feel to it altogether. Her second picture is more provocative and suggestive. Like Matt's image with his girlfriend, the shadows make it very hard to see her face, thus even further highlighting her body. These shadowed images are interesting to me because they are not "good" photographs in a traditional sense. Yet, these images remain because they serve a purpose—for Matt the shadows keep the emphasis on his girlfriend, while for Carly (Figure 1.8) the emphasis remains on her body.

In contrast Peter, a twelfth-grade boy, depicts the self in a different way in his timeline and album images (Figure 1.9). This is not a close-up picture, and between the lighting and image quality, it is hard to really see what he looks like. When I asked him about this image, Peter told me that he thought this was a flattering picture of him. While his image is not focused on the body, it signals several important things about the self to his dual audience; in particular, his socioeconomic status, which is evident in the car and his clothing. This is Peter in the context of consumerism. The marking of social class was evident in many of the highlights reel pictures; girls often emphasized clothing in their images, whether it be a designer product or a pair of very trendy shoes (during the study Sperry shoes were extremely popular and I saw several images of girls' feet wearing the brand's styles), while boys often had pictures in or in front of fancy cars. Both boys and girls often highlighted travel experiences as well. This was a source of great frustration for several of the teens. Kenny, who noted that his family does not have the opportunity to go on "fancy vacations," reported that many guys post pictures

> like on a Nantucket beach showing that you have more money than someone else. Like I come from [a small town], I uh, I went to vacation in third grade to Disney world. And like 10 kids from my grade went to Atlantis [this year]. Uh a bunch of kids went to Ultra Music Festival in Miami over break. Kids go to, all over the world. And I'm just at home like "sick guys" . . . I see their photos.

Figure 1.8 Carly's Bikini Picture

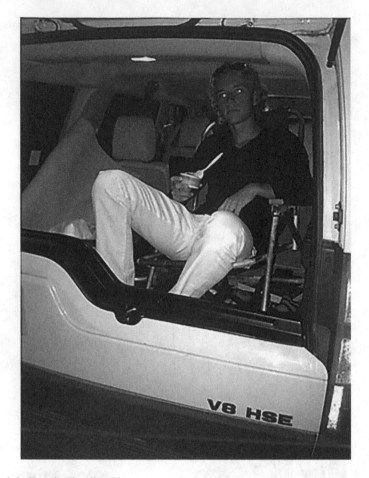

Figure 1.9 Peter's Timeline Picture

The visible signs of class and consumerism may be more prominent among these teens given that most live in and/or attend schools in middle- to upper-class areas of the country; however, I think it is important to note here that for this group of teens, signaling class was a component of the self that appeared often in photographs.

There were a few boys[5] who clearly eschewed this model, opting to post pictures that seemed intentionally unflattering. Noah hardly ever posts his own pictures to his Facebook and began our interview saying, "I don't post very much on Facebook; you might have noticed." After we discussed the fact that some people post everything about their day, including their breakfast cereal, he said, "You're probably thinking I'm kind of antisocial because I don't post that many things." When I asked him if this was the case, if he would describe himself as "antisocial," he said, "Yeah that could be true."

Here we can see some of the self-narrative work that is often masked by these surface presentations. Noah assumes that the impression given off (Goffman 1959) by his social media presentation is that he is antisocial, and he tests this theory out on me early in our interview. His comment that this "could be true" indicates that he is working through this self-conception on two levels—first, he is questioning if others equate limited social media use with antisocial tendencies as he thinks and second, he seems to be testing whether he thinks he fits this antisocial label. Noah is an interesting case of someone who was very quick to critique others for focusing too much on "branding" themselves on social media, and he made it clear to me that he feels he is one of the few people who present a genuine presentation of the self. He typically posts images that would not be considered a highlights reel—goofy shots in which he either looks bored or really intense. While he does post a few pictures with friends, particularly a few with "hot girls," and travel, most of his pictures are individual shots that are either unclear without context or not typically flattering in appearance and presentation of the self. When I asked him about this, he said, "I figure the way I look in the picture is probably the way I look in real life." This really is Noah's fable; over the course of the interview it became clear that his personal fable is all about being real and taking pride in his perceived antisocial tendencies. For him, the impression that he is developing on Facebook highlights his authenticity and lack of concern about his image. Yet, at the same time, he is still crafting a highlights reel, it is just one that looks very different from his peers'. His presentation of the self still fits his personal fable and his own version of how to "document us being awesome." Noah's is an example where the presentation looks very different, but the self-work underneath the presentation is the same as his peers.

The teens also used pictures from plays, performances, and athletics to document the self on their timelines. I observed a few pictures, such as one of Chris' hockey pictures, which showcases his entire team celebrating on the ice after a big win. We can infer that they are celebrating because they are all doing the "throw up the one" pose, as the boys labeled it, which indicates athletic success. This picture received 16 likes, and Chris' comment on this picture, "fucking right boys," is directed to his fellow teammates. This is the highlights reel in all its masculine glory.

However, beyond these few celebratory images of big tournament wins or the new team picture that gets posted each season, for the most part the team is noticeably absent in the athletic pictures that participants, both boys and girls, posted. In many cases, although the teens are engaged in team sports, they have chosen either to select images that do not highlight the team, or have cropped teammates out altogether. In Lilah's picture (Figure 1.10) we see her perform, but we do not see her team or opponent.

This focus on the individual in sports pictures surprised me, as I had initially thought there would be more status inferred from pictures like Chris' hockey team picture. I assumed that to be seen in the context of other equally athletic peers would give you both athletic and social cache. Yet this hypothesis did not hold for the teens I met. What I came to understand from talking to these teens is that the individual sports picture still offers a lot for the highlights reel; these

Figure 1.10 Lilah's Track Picture

images allow the teens to signal, and in a way perhaps overemphasize, their athletic contributions. In these images, the teens appear to be in control and dominating athletically, yet we honestly have no idea if this is the truth; we do not see competitors, scores, or how the teen compares physically or athletically with his or her teammates. The individual shot removes the larger context, which allows them to signal their awesomeness on the field without running the risk of being compared to others who may be fitter or better. This provides an important safety net for the ideal self.

Conclusion

Adolescents do not begin the social media creation phase as blank slates, ready to create or shape a performance of the self. Rather, because the public and private are intertwined (Jurgenson and Rey 2012), their social media experiences can best be understood as visual microcosms of the self. In the survey, 92 percent of participants reported that social media is integrated into their daily lives and said that they do not see social media, in this case primarily Facebook and Instagram, as separate from everyday offline life. Interestingly, the two girls who said they view social media as a separate online reality were the two girls who posted the most provocative and revealing pictures, both in terms of sexualized images of the body and risk behaviors (alcohol and nicotine consumption). But aside from these two cases, these teens are not using social media to have anonymous conversations or create an alternate persona. As used, these social media sites/apps do not allow them to break free from the social constraints of day-to-day life; rather, because they bring their experiences, peer group, and social status to social media, their challenges and strengths offline become their challenges and strengths online. As a result, they are engaged in creating a public personal fable on social media. This narrative is created in their minds and then made public and visual on social media.

The adolescents I interviewed negotiated this by engaging in highly strategic impression management work. While some momentary lapses in judgment can be seen in the images I observed, for the most part the adolescents reported very thoughtful and rational reasons for selecting certain images. As adult observers, we may cringe at the content of the images and wish that teens did not feel the need to show party pictures or bikini pictures. Nonetheless, the level of strategy that they employ, coupled with the time and emotional investment they make on social media, means that online impression management is a controlled effort for them.

Interestingly, most teens simultaneously refer to their social media presentation as the "real me" but also acknowledge that, like any photo album we keep, social media largely represents the "highlights reel" of their experiences, relationships, and appearance. This discrepancy is not troubling to them, and indeed there is nothing about the highlights reel that is inauthentic. While it might not represent every facet of the individual, neither do their offline front stage performances in school, at home, at work, or with friends.

Ultimately, what gets presented in the highlights reel, particularly in the all-important profile pictures, is the surface self. This emphasis on the surface self in profile pictures becomes more substantive when looking at the timeline images and photo albums that make up the overall profile, but the profile photo—the first impression—largely emphasizes appearance and friends. This impression work is guided by a set of social media rules, many of which I have hinted at in this chapter. These rules are critical because they bound the presentation that adolescents give and also serve as a way to mark symbolic boundaries and social categories of worth. I will explore this in greater detail in the next chapter.

When taken as a collective whole, the presentation of the self on social media in the profile picture, cover photos, and timeline/album pictures is varied. At times, particularly in their profile pictures, teens are following the patterns that they see around them. This is what Marie did with her prom picture, as it mirrored her peers' images, and in many ways this guarantees a positive response. It is in these moments that the highlights can feel, to some viewers, cliché. But at other times, particularly in the timeline and album pictures, teens showed real diversity in their documentation of the self in their images. As a whole, these were less stylized and generic. This back-and-forth movement between collective identity and independence is what defines adolescence; it is marked by moments of testing the boundaries and then alternately playing it safe. Some, like Noah, are willing to push the boundaries more often than others, but they are all testing them and learning in the process.

Notes

1 Interestingly, many participants spoke of seeing people post their college rejection letters on social media. Although I did not witness this in the feeds of my participants, I think this loss of face in one realm (academics) is counterbalanced by the value it has in asserting group belonging and cohesion. This sends the message that the poster is just like everyone else as well as signaling that he or she can find humor in his or her rejections.
2 Matt reported that he does not care about looking good because he has a long-term girlfriend and therefore felt that it does not matter for him. Noah, a twelfth-grade boy who began his interview by asking if I thought he was "antisocial on Facebook," made a concerted effort to challenge Facebook norms and intentionally posts images that are not flattering.
3 While none of the boys in the study changed their profile pictures to a red equal sign to indicate their support for marriage equality, in general they were more likely than the girls to include political images, links, or status updates in their news feeds. They just did not do this in their profile pictures. In general, though, they changed their profile pictures far less frequently than the girls in the study.
4 Bathroom mirror selfies are pictures in which the person points the camera at the bathroom mirror to take a picture. It can be a group or individual shot, and I observed it only among female participants. You can often see the flash from the camera in the picture, and most often these are posed and stylized pictures.
5 There was one girl who wavered between the two, sometimes posting flattering images and sometimes posting unflattering images to intentionally mock her peers who are so outwardly focused on appearance. Her choices are more strategic and less clear cut than the other examples in this section. As such, her story will be explored more fully in the final chapter.

References

Cooley, Charles. 1964. *Human Nature and the Social Order*. New York, NY: Scribner's.
Davis, Jenny. 2014. "Triangulating the Self: Identity Processes in a Connected Era" *Symbolic Interaction* 37: 500–523.
Entwistle, Joanne and Ashley Mears. 2012. "Gender on Display: Performativity in Fashion Modelling" *Cultural Sociology* 7: 320–335.
Elkind, David. 1967. "Egocentrism in Adolescence" *Child Development* 38: 1025–1034.
Goffman, Erving. 1955. "On Face-Work: An Analysis of Ritual Elements in Social Interaction" *Psychiatry: Journal for the Study of Interpersonal Processes* 18: 213–231.

————. 1959. *The Presentation of Self in Everyday Life*. New York, NY: Anchor Books, Doubleday.

Hogan, Bernie. 2010. "The Presentation of Self in the Age of Social Media: Distinguishing Performances and Exhibitions Online" *Bulletin of Science, Technology, and Society* 30: 377–386.

Jurgenson, Nathan and P.J. Rey. 2012. "The Fan Dance: How Privacy Thrives in an Age of Cyber-Publicity" in *Unlike Us Reader: Social Media Monopolies and Their Alternatives,* edited by Geert Lovink and Miriam Rasch. Amsterdam: Institute of Network Cultures.

Kramer, Nicole and Stephen Winter. 2008. "Impression Management 2.0: The Relationship of Self-Esteem, Extroversion, Self-Efficacy, and Self-Presentation Within Social Networking Sites" *Journal of Media Psychologies* 20: 106–116.

Turkle, Sherry. 2011. *Alone Together: Why We Expect More From Technology and Less From Each Other*. New York, NY: Basic Books.

Zhao, Shanyang, Sherri Grasmuck, and Jason Martin. 2008. "Identity Construction on Facebook: Digital Empowerment in Anchored Relationships" *Computers in Human Behavior* 24: 1816–1836.

2 Facebook rules and boundary demarcation

Presenting their ideal personal fable on Facebook is important to teens, but there are rules that guide this process, and adolescents both adhere to them and monitor their peers' adherence to them. If social media is the toolkit for the self in dialogue that exists on social media, these social norms are the instructions for how to use the tools. These rules provide a framework for teens' impression management work, but importantly they are simply guides, not requirements. Just as some people will read the instruction manual for their new phone in great detail, others will skim for the key points, and others still will promptly discard the instructions, opting to sort it out themselves. The same thing is true of these adolescents and their adherence to the social media rules. Still, following these rules is important because it ensures that group belonging is solidified; or at the very least it ensures that you are not out of the group. Teens want to make sure that their images will be liked and appreciated by their peer group; if they violate the rules, it will be harder for them to find peer acceptance for their images. Additionally, if everyone is following the rules in the group, the images will look similar, almost giving the group a sort of feel or tone. Many teens told me they can tell friendship groups based on the similarities of the images. This is not necessarily a negative thing, as it allows them to visually confirm their answer to the "where do I fit in" question.

Assuring social belonging is critical to teens and their conceptions of the self. Once belonging is established, they can do the work to determine how well, and in what ways, they fit the group. For example, how is it that their social media style can be very similar to their friends' in spite of the fact that they have different interests? Do they like that it matches or not? Does it even matter to them? The notion that the self can be understood and evaluated by understanding one's social belonging and position in the group echoes Erikson's (1980) conceptualization of the ways that adolescents navigate collective and individual identity work. The self is bounded by rules, but even in following the rules teens are free to explore the self. Once group membership is established via the rules, teens have an opportunity to explore the pathways and processes of understanding the self. In following the rules they can develop a deeper understanding of the parts of themselves that fit, or do not fit, with a social group.

Additionally, the rules serve as a safety net. The teens I spoke with rely on these rules because they reduce unknowns; without these guidelines, impression management work on Facebook would be far more risky, as it would be hard to know how images or comments will be interpreted. Although to be sure, the rules are not foolproof, as many can still be hard to interpret and execute. But for the most part, knowing and following the rules enables teens to ensure that their presentation of self is not misinterpreted by their peers. While some rules are universal, it is important to note that social groups can create their own rules, which they adhere to as a form of boundary maintenance. The social group rules are more difficult for me to assess as I did not speak to many teens within the same peer group, but they referenced them often enough in the interviews that it was clear that they are keeping track of both universal and specific rules on social media. The specific rules were often evident in the interviews with the girls; I showed each girl who participated in the study two bikini pictures (the subjects of the pictures were unknown to them) with very different tones in order to check the validity of my image coding. Interestingly, most girls said things like, "That might be what she and her friends do, but my friends all . . ." or "My friends would totally think that is . . ." Their comments imply that though there are local cultures and norms on social media, there is some leeway for violating the norms. After all, they recognized that not everyone would do things the same way they do. This same sense of perspective or empathy was not extended to their school peers or friends, all of whom they felt should know and follow the rules appropriately.

A quick note here: I am calling these rules "universal" because they were universal for my participants, regardless of age, gender, school, and race. However, because my sample was so small, I do not assume that these rules apply to all teens equally, and indeed I believe there may be some particularly interesting differences at the intersection of race and gender, which my data cannot address. As such, the specific rules that are described here may not be relevant to *all* teens. However, while the rules may look different, my discussions with these teens indicate that the functions of the rules and the ways in which they are enacted and policed will likely be very similar. This is an area rich for further research.

The teens I interviewed made it clear that those who violate the rules face some social consequences. While social media cannot improve teens' offline social standing, according to my interviewees, violating the rules can hurt them socially. One of my participants experienced this four years prior to our interview and felt that he was still suffering socially. Thus, rule following can create in-group and out-group boundaries. Those who post pictures that do not follow rules are considered "weird" or "losers" by the larger group. In this way, the rules create social categories of worth (Steensland 2006) between those who understand and follow these rules and those who cannot or chose not.

For some, rule following is almost a holding pattern. Some of the teens I met were content to stay inside the rules, focusing primarily on the group conformity phase of self-development, and by making sure that their pictures fit they group they generally ensured that they were well received by their peers. Others moved beyond the rules to focus on their self-development and individuality, with less concern about the group, and often a willingness to ignore or challenge the rules. Others did a little of both—conforming in some pictures and testing out the self in other images. These teens' rule-following practices seem similar to their developmental processes in that they are all in different places.

The rules of facebook

Some of the rules are very obvious. Others are less so. Some apply to everyone in the same way, and others are enacted differently by males and females. (The gendered component of the rules is very important, and will be the focus of Chapter 3.) While the teens made it clear that it is important to follow the rules, they do not always understand the reasons for them or agree on what they mean. For example, while almost every girl in the study had a picture in which she was doing the "duck face" pose—pouting with puckered lips drawn forward like a kiss or duckbill—few could explain the origin of the duck face or its purpose.

The only answer I received about the purpose of the duck face came during my interview with Tom, an 18-year-old boy who has a long-term girlfriend. Tom said the duck face

> pulls your face, so if you have like a chin that you don't like. . . Or if you have like your cheeks are too big or something, it pulls your face forward. . . So it looks like you have sunken cheeks, it looks like your skin's almost flawless.

Tom's explanation is that the "duck face" is popular because it gives the illusion of a slimmer and more "flawless" face, which made sense given the intense focus on appearance among the girls. I asked several girls to assess Tom's answer, and they responded, "Is that what it is?" or "Really?" They did not necessarily agree or disagree with Tom; they really had no idea. While there is certainly not a duck face rule on social media, there are many rules about appearance and what constitutes looking good. When girls look at other girls' images and see that they all have a "duck face" photo, it becomes something they feel they should have. The fact that the girls did not know the reason for the "duck face" does not negate their importance. We conform to norms all the time without being conscious of the meanings embedded in them (Berger and Luckmann 1966).

Authenticity bounded by the rules

How is authenticity bounded by Facebook rules and norms? All of the teens made it clear that it is not acceptable to fabricate social situations or events to create a hoped-for highlights reel. However, while they spoke about showing their "real" selves, it was never truly the case that they revealed everything about themselves. Although it is important to note that this is true in all of our interactions. Adolescents present on social media what can be best described as a strategic and evolving authenticity. It is strategic in its adherence to the rules and evolving in the sense that it changes as the adolescent makes decisions about how closely to follow the rules and what constitutes his or her highlights reel. And of course, it evolves as their answers to the questions of where do I fit in and who am I change as well.

Cassie, a ninth-grade girl, mentioned repeatedly in her interview that her images are very real and was very quick to point out that she does not worry about the number of likes she receives. Yet when I asked her to describe the story of her images and why she selected them for social media, she could explain exactly how her images serve specific purposes for her. When I asked her if there are certain types of images that girls should have, she said that there were no expectations or rules, but then went on to lay out the guidelines she follows:

> There's not like a certain array, that each person has to have, it's not like, it's not like there's a sheet a paper. . . checklist. But, I mean for me I definitely have to have pictures with my friends, I have to have a few artsy pictures. Um, I don't know it just shows like your feminine side. And then, oh yeah I mean some girls, I mean the girls who are really like, really, really feminine, um don't need this but I mean I, in particular, I'm like really, really centered around um sports, too. So I have sports pictures, I mean I don't have like, like guys like a Boston Bruins' logo but I have me and my team, and that's kind of like a mixture between friends and um. . . sports so it works out.

Cassie begins by saying that there is no "checklist" of required pictures; however, she then says, "for me I definitely have to have," which indicates that she is operating from a set of guidelines for her presentation of the self. These may not be universal, but they do seem to guide Cassie's presentation. Most strikingly, Cassie indicates that it is important for her to have "artsy" pictures, (i.e., bathroom mirror selfies or the photo shoot pictures alluded to in the last chapter) in order to show her "feminine side" because she is "really centered around um sports." Cassie understands the impressions that her images give off, and there are rules, at least as Cassie interprets them, about the balance between feminine images and those she deems less feminine, in this case her sports pictures. Cassie has many artsy photo shoot pictures in her timeline that she uses to offset the athletic image she may project in school, or in the many soccer pictures she was tagged in during the fall season in which I interviewed her. She can try out these aspects of what she deems the more feminine self on social media; she can play with them, discard them, or adopt them as she sees fit. With her team sports pictures she can confirm a group membership with her teammates and then present a different side of herself with the "girly" images she creates for her social media. These images represent components of the real Cassie—at least as she conceptualizes herself in this moment. Cassie wants to present both of these sides of herself, and social media allows her to do so in a way that she can control. And again, because she believes these to be authentic, they are meaningful for her in this way.

Cassie's example reveals both the generality and specificity of social media rules; there are rules, such as those regarding gender, that seemed to be universally accepted by the majority of participants, however it was also the case that most participants internalized and expressed these rules in specific and individual ways. For example, while all participants agreed that there were certain pictures that girls "typically" had in their feed (perhaps images with friends), each girl will follow the rules in her own specific way, thus leading to a sense of common images with individual style and execution. The remainder of the chapter will focus on the general rules that the participants agreed upon, and the examples will reflect the specific ways these teens embody these rules. It is important to formally describe these rules here, because all of the teens I interviewed told me that while the rules guide their image selections (to ensure that they fit group expectations), they rarely speak to friends or peers about these rules. They learn them socially by observing peers' images or by watching the fallout when others violate the rules; these are rules that are socially intuited.

Rule #1: likes mark your social belonging

Although they are not images, likes are an important part of the visual narrative, as they accompany pictures and offer some understanding about how others see the image and potentially the poster as well. Likes are very important to all teens because they serve as important visual markers of belonging. I intentionally use the term "social belonging" instead of "status" as teens were adamant in explaining that popularity is only a component of who/what gets likes on Facebook. While popular people do get a lot of likes, they get them mostly from their social group, which is also what happens for teens with less social status, it is just that the popular kids have a wider social network from which to draw these likes. Likes tell the audience that the poster is connected to a social group. Likes do not determine your friendships, but rather likes are visible representations of your friendships and social group. And interestingly, a few girls reported that, with the exception of their very close friends' images, which they will like as soon as they are posted regardless of who else has liked them in a manner of reciprocal liking (i.e., I like my friend's image and she in turn will like my image as soon as I post it), they often look first at the other people who have liked the image before deciding to like it themselves. Lucy, a chatty 18-year-old girl who spoke lightning fast and in full paragraphs, said that she will only like things that her friends have already liked because she does not want to be the first person to like it. When I asked her about this, she said that if people have not liked the image already, it may mean that "maybe it is unlikable." Inherently the number of likes may signal the value of the image or poster. For Lucy, being one of the people who likes the image is also a way to signal social belonging; she wants to like what her friends like and does in some way view their likes, or lack thereof, as an indication of the image's likability. Thus the correlation people often make between likes and popularity is not necessarily totally accurate; all participants acknowledged that you can get likes for things other than being popular. As Lucy commented,

> Well, like on Facebook, certain people who will get a lot of likes and stuff, which I think is the main thing, like that person's popular, but it's also like certain. . . people will get likes for different things, and from their group of friends. . . I guess it depends on what you mean by popular, like some people might say popular is being really cool and stuff, but also it could be someone who has a lot of friends, so I mean. . .

It is clear Lucy is wrestling with definitions of popularity and what likes can or cannot contribute to this, which indicates one of the challenges embedded in the architecture of the like: on the surface it has become a shorthand way to signal popularity, but it can mean many other things. The like can also signal "I was here too" as some teens called it. They are connected by association. Generally speaking, the people in the picture or people who were in the know (either of the event, social context, etc.) will like the picture. Thus, the like can provide a visual signal of social belonging to both the giver and the receiver of the like. While likes are in theory a way to signal social belonging by accumulation, they may be signals for the giver as well the receiver of the like.

While likes were important to all participants, and indeed all of them were extremely accurate in recalling exactly how many likes they received for the images we discussed in our interviews, boys and girls do experience them differently. In the focus groups, girls indicated that they are looking for a fairly specific number of likes. They wanted more than 20 likes on their profile picture; between 10–20 likes was considered acceptable but not great; and they told me that getting less than four likes was a disaster. And again, girls expect that their friends will all like their images regardless of what they post (generally speaking) because giving likes is just a component of being a good friend. In contrast, boys, with a few rare exceptions, did not receive as many likes as the girls, nor did they give as many likes. During the focus group, the boys joked about the number of likes that girls get and acknowledged that they come nowhere close. One said that "more girls look at likes" and another said that he will "see girls that have like 200 likes on their profile picture." There was some debate about whether they paid more attention to girls with more likes (i.e., did the likes indicate these girls might be worth paying more attention to because others did?), but they ultimately agreed that they think girls are less genuine in giving likes. As one boy said, "Sorry, I just feel like the girls do it in a much more fake way, I would say, like they like each other's (pictures) . . . they'll comment, 'Oh you're so pretty,' if guys did that, it would be really, really weird." They then joked with each other, saying, "You look handsome, man," and "it's a nice photo of you, Tom," to great laughter from the group. In my interview with Max, one of the 18-year-old boys in his senior spring semester, he told me that posting an image just to get likes is "pardon my French, but that's like a whore." For Max this type of behavior feels transactional—you are doing something only to have the external validation of the like—and ultimately Max believes that the poster is selling some version of him or herself to get likes. And while girls were willing to like their friends' content with relative ease, they were aware of certain images being selected just to get likes. They were generally dismissive of this behavior. It is interesting to consider this idea of posting images just to get likes in the context of their emphasis on authenticity. They all want to get likes, but somehow the likes have to be perceived as authentic, not bought, to use Max's analogy.

While boys may be dismissive of the number of girls' likes, when boys described their pictures to me, they often referenced the number of likes they received. When I asked Jake to tell me the story of his profile picture, an image of him on stage receiving his diploma, he began by talking about likes, both the fact that he was not posting for likes and to acknowledge the high number he received, saying, "Like I wasn't posting it for likes, well I got, I was surprised actually with like how many people liked it. It was cool." While he is sure to say that he did not post the picture specifically to get likes, alluding to Max's notion of being a "whore" for likes, he does begin his discussion of the picture by talking about likes and saying that the large number he received was "cool." This is especially telling as I never asked him about likes, but rather asked him to describe the picture. When I followed up and asked him specifically about the likes, he said, "I don't care, some people care." In the unguarded moment of describing his image, Jake revealed that he thought it was "cool" to get so many likes, however when asked directly about likes he sticks with the gendered norms that indicate boys should not visibly care about receiving social approval. These and other rules around masculinity will be outlined more fully in the next chapter, but is important to note that while the numbers may be different for boys and girls, likes matter for everyone.

Given the precision with which they could remember the number of likes their images received and the cutoffs the girls had established about the number of likes they needed/wanted to get, I was surprised by how few likes these teens actually received on their pictures. Many of the participants did not receive the number of likes that they said that they expected or hoped for, and there was a clear range within the data. The difference between the interview presentation and the real numbers was particularly striking for the girls. The average girl's picture received 1–10 likes. Some girls received 11–20 likes, but very few had more than that (remember that they defined 10–20 likes as acceptable, but not ideal, and less than four was considered a disaster). And many pictures, particularly boys' pictures, had no likes at all.

This was unexpected and has several possible explanations. First, there is a distinct difference in the number of likes participants receive for profile pictures versus an album or timeline picture, and perhaps participants were thinking only of their profile pictures when they made the statements in the interview about likes. Profile pictures receive far more likes, but over the course of the two-week period far fewer profile pictures were posted than timeline or album pictures (these teens seemed to keep their profile pictures for at least a week or so), which would naturally lower the average during my observation. I do not believe this explains the phenomenon entirely, as the profile pictures also had fewer likes in general than they indicated.

Another possible reason for this may be that girls inflated the numbers of likes they received when we talked about it in the focus groups. For example, the group of girls aged 15–18 talked about how bad it is to get less than 20 likes on profile pictures, however three out of the 12 girls in that group had profile pictures that received less than 20 likes. Because I had no sense of what the range would be at the point of the focus group, I asked them, and wonder if this had the unintended effect of silencing those who received fewer likes. The higher numbers given could have been inflated for the benefit of the others in the group or simply represent one end of what is really a range of acceptable number of likes. I did follow up in the interviews to see if these numbers still felt accurate, but it is possible that participants may have been unwilling to challenge the numbers in an effort to save face. Whatever the reason, very few of my participants actually hit the likes target mentioned in the focus groups.

In addition to showing that you are part of the group, likes also serve as a visual symbol of how the group evaluates you. Essentially, likes become a form of social media friend feedback. And interestingly, likes from those just outside their circle of close friends appeared to be the most meaningful form of feedback. Likes from potential romantic partners obviously matter a lot, which will be explored more in the next section, but for now the point is that boys told me that they pay very close attention to girls who like their images, and girls also reported that they notice likes from boys more than those from their close friends. One note here: the majority of my participants identified as heterosexual and as such, the examples here largely reflect opposite sex romantic relationships. This will be covered in greater detail in the next chapter. One boy said that when a girl likes a picture "you're like, 'Wait does she like me? Is this a message?'" He said that one like might not mean anything, so you "got to see if it's like something consistent sometimes." One like from a girl could legitimately mean that she just likes the picture, but liking multiple images may be a hint. And they are definitely paying attention!

Overall, boys and girls both reported that likes from someone just beyond their close social circle are especially interesting. As one 18-year-old girl said, "likes outside your [social] group register more." While friends may like things simply because of reciprocity norms in friendship (i.e., I just like everything my friend posts), likes from those just outside the circle may be less common and therefore may be more likely to register as specific feedback. In essence, these are the people who do not *have to* like your pictures, and therefore the fact that they do like them may be meaningful.

Although the like is a simple thumbs-up icon, these teens give it a more specific meaning; they saw it as a positive assessment of something specific—it could be that they are attractive, popular, fun/funny, or were involved in something great. Amala, a ninth-grade girl who does not have social media but observes vicariously through friends and her older sister's account, talked about likes at length. She said, "I don't know, I think [likes] just makes you feel good about yourself I guess. . . . If you get more, then people, people like you, people think you're pretty or whatever." At the very least, likes are a positive indicator of how well you perform the surface front stage impression management of signaling attractiveness and likability. While Amala talks about likes indicating that you look pretty, Amala was also very clear that girls are not trying to look "model" pretty, rather the emphasis is on looking "pretty for you," whatever that may be.

While Amala was 13 at the time of the study, many of the older teens gave appropriately more nuanced explanations for likes. In addition to signaling attractiveness and likability, likes also can give a thumbs-up to an image or event, irrespective of the person. Finally, they told me about the "sarcastic like," which, just as it sounds, is really the opposite of a like. Sarcastic likes are used to mock the person posting the image or comment and send a sarcastic signal to those who see it. As Jake notes, these "sarcastic likes" are common and can be perceived as funny or mean depending on the context. When I asked Jake if the sarcastic like can be a coded way to indicate that you really do not like the person, he responded with a laugh: "I do that all the time."

Sarcastic likes can be as obvious as a "cool kid" liking a "loser's" image, but they also can be more subtle. Max was very honest in acknowledging that he has received sarcastic likes, saying (in an appropriately sarcastic tone) that he gets them "all the time. Those are great." When I asked how he knows they are sarcastic likes, he explained,

> Some of my quote unquote "most popular posts" were the ones where like, [I captioned it] "Got hit by a car on a bike," or, "Got two flats on a bike ride," or like, "Ran into a tree," or this one time I biked off a cliff and I, and it was like a ten-foot ledge, but you know, "I'm gonna kill myself."

Though sarcastic likes in this context were not deeply troubling to Max, he knew that some of his pictures that "do the best" on social media (i.e., have the most likes) are the result of people liking his mistakes.

While a like from a good friend and a like for falling off a cliff may both be easy to interpret, most of the teens spoke about how hard it is in general to interpret likes, and many, particularly boys, confessed that they sometimes have a hard time determining the tone of the like. Is it a sarcastic like, and if so, is it a friendly joke or an expression of subtle meanness? Additionally, it is sometimes confusing why certain people, often those not directly connected with a picture, like it. Some of the teens described posting images that they believed would resonate with a certain audience only to get likes from people outside that group. As one boy said, "I get really confused as to why [some] people liked it."

While the meaning of the like can be confusing, the person who gives the like also can complicate matters more if the recipient does not understand their connection or interest. After Jake listed all the possible meanings for likes, I asked him how he knows he interprets his likes correctly. He told me, "It's very confusing. It's very confusing." When I asked if he ends up having to just guess in some cases, he said, "Yeah kind of. . . If it's with a girl you know, sometimes I'll message her, and just see how that goes. Sometimes it goes well, sometimes it doesn't. I mean, it's just one of those things where you have to guess." Gebre talked about his confusion with likes, noting that it is especially strange for him when he posts status updates in other languages and will get likes from friends who literally cannot understand what he wrote. He described it as "How can you even understand this?" I wondered out loud with Gebre about why people might like things that they cannot understand, and he could not articulate an explanation for this. He did not see this as a status marker (people liking it because they think he is cool or because of the other people that have liked it; in this case those people are largely unknown to them given the language barrier). He really just did not get it. For many of the teens, the positive thumbs-up of the like can be just as confusing as the negative feedback.

Though Jake and other teens may sometimes be confused about a like's meaning, this lack of clarity does nothing to diminish the power of the likes. According to Berger and Luckmann (1966), meaning can be derived without true understanding of a phenomenon; what is important is not so much what the thing means, but rather the fact that one designates it as "expressing meaning" (129). To illustrate this, Berger and Luckmann (1966) give the example of someone laughing; we may not understand what the person is laughing at, but we know that his laughter is an expression of happiness, which makes it meaningful to us. I believe this same concept is at work with social media likes; while teens may not always be able to define their precise meaning, they know that likes are meaningful because they signal something positive about their social belonging and serve as evaluative feedback from peers. And this feedback may be targeted at the personal fable these teens are working to create.

Rule #2: images, not words, signal your "highlights reel"

All the teens said that they cannot verbally boast about themselves on Facebook as this would be viewed as showing off. To get around this and still show the highlights reel, they use images to signal their successes; thus they are highlighting their achievements visually "while hiding the labor of doing so" (Davis 2014: 6). While you cannot say that you are awesome, you are allowed to use images to "document" the awesome without violating social norms. This is not to say that all images are acceptable, and indeed an image is not risk free (many of the teens described certain images as signaling that the poster is "trying too hard" to be awesome), but for many teens it is safer to signal something with an image rather than to say it outright. This is an example of Goffman's notion of creating a "given off impression"; an image creates an opportunity for a positive overall impression to be "given off" by the poster (Goffman 1959; Davis 2012).

Sports, travel, physical appearance, relationship status, and "cool events" or experiences are just a few of the things that can be shown through images in ways that are far more socially acceptable than writing status updates that describe these same successes. Bikini pictures clearly show everyone that the girl is slim without her having to announce it. Sports pictures can also show triumphs or accomplishments, and for the boys they can also highlight aspects of traditional masculinity, particularly when they showcase athletic success. An example of this is the ice hockey picture of Chris described earlier, in which all of the boys on the team are holding up their index finger in a gesture to indicate that they are number one. They are league champions, but no one has to write this, least of all Chris. He can post this image and have it signal his team membership, athletic success, and masculinity.

Both boys and girls in the study said that they have used likes to signal that they are interested in someone romantically. These likes feel safe to them because likes can mean so many different things that they do not feel that they are really putting themselves out there in an obvious way that might risk rejection. Indeed, many kids told me it is "easier to break the ice" on social media, so really the like may be the first nudge. Likes can be used to engage in subtle flirting and allow the person to gauge the response before moving on to a more personal form of communication. Several teens, both male and female, said that they would start with a like and/or comment on a picture and then, if they received a positive response, they may move on to Facebook messaging, then texting, and finally flirting in person. Thus Facebook likes can be the first step towards signaling potential romantic interest and establishing more contact.

This is just a small sampling of the signaling that images provide on social media. Images can be used to depict many attributes of the personal fable that would be socially unacceptable to boast about in words. They create the overall "given off" impression of the person's highlights (Goffman 1959). The important information that you want others to know about your projected self can be transmitted.

Rule #3: don't talk about social media

In talking with participants in focus groups and interviews, it was clear that they rarely talk offline about the day-to-day social media experiences they have or see on social media. Let me be clear here; they talk about social media *all* the time, but this group of teens did not talk in great detail with their peers about the little things—how they interpreted likes, what to do about the small social slights they incur, or the confusions about how to read the image. While a major violation of the rules or an amazing experience, such as a picture with a celebrity, would be a topic of in-person conversation, day-to-day social media experiences are not usually discussed offline in a substantive way.

I am wary to use the terms "online" and "offline," as this gives the impression that teens operate in two separate worlds. As stated in the introduction, this is a false dichotomy. Davis (2013) offers an interesting alternative to this terminology. She suggests that we think of teens as always online as long as they are "maintaining a presence" online. By this she means that if you can reach them online via their social media accounts, they are online, even if they are not then physically logged on at the moment—they still exist online. I agree with Davis; this work that I describe as the self in dialogue is happening all the time, regardless of whether they are logged on to their social media account or not. I was surprised that these teens do not talk specifically about those logged-in moments in person; I assumed that given the time and energy they put into social media, it would permeate more of their conversations. Virtually all participants, regardless of age and gender, disagreed. They said that they do not talk about their logged-in social media experiences (this differs from their pre-posting engagement with peers, which is an exception to this rule, particularly for girls; I address this in the next paragraph) with their friends or ask their friends about theirs, opting instead to interpret and internalize their experiences privately. Again, there are exceptions: breaking news, a fight that plays out on social media, breakups, new flirtations, and so forth. But for the day-to-day mundane postings, these teens reported that they do not discuss them.

There are some gender differences in the extent to which this is upheld. Boys said that they hardly ever talk about social media with their peers (barring a major piece of gossip or mistake); they select images, post comments or likes, and judge their responses without consultation from others. Virtually all boys, with the exception of those who acknowledged receiving initial help setting up an account from an older relative, had no help or advice in adding content to their Facebook. When I asked if they discussed social media with their friends, they said that barring one of the big events mentioned above, they would not bring it up face-to-face. In contrast, girls, to varying degrees, will talk about all aspects of creating their social media (i.e., selecting images) with their friends until they actually post their pictures. Once the picture is posted, it becomes a more private experience. Many girls said that they have experienced slights on social media—everything from mean comments/screenshots of private content that gets forwarded on, to being cropped out of pictures, to realizing a group of friends hung out without them—yet when I asked if they ever discussed it with their friends in person, they all said no.

This indicates that the process of making meaning around their social media experiences is largely an individual process. This may be because this is part of the self in dialogue work of figuring out the emerging authentic self, which need not be shared, or there may be something about their social media experiences that makes it difficult to translate into face-to-face discussions. I think, too, there is a desire to avoid confrontation, as most girls said that they would avoid saying things to smooth over social relationships rather than confront things directly. Either way, this creates a fascinating scenario: teens externalize the personal fable to hundreds of their social media friends but then have this very private experience of reacting to and interpreting the feedback experience alone.

This potentially could have negative consequences for teens who are bullied on social media and then do not share their experiences with others or ask for help, particularly because they are always "maintaining a presence" (Davis 2013). And even in the cases of kids who are not bullied per se, but reported seeing images on social media that left them feeling either excluded or hurt, there can be negative consequences. Especially interesting here is the fact that similarly they do not ask for help or share experiences. This could lead to feelings of isolation and the false sense that others do not have these experiences. These negative effects are important to acknowledge and have been well documented in the literature.

But for the teens who are not bullied, these solo processing experiences of self-evaluation can be positive. Samantha, a twelfth-grade girl, spoke about how being alone when she processes Facebook feedback actually is freeing for her:

> I think it's probably because like. . . maybe it's just cause they can't see. . . their reaction. Like say they don't respond, you don't have to deal with them [to your face] yeah. It's just like they don't respond, but it's not like you have to look at and watch them. . . I mean you do, but they don't see your reaction

to their reaction. It's just sort of safer because you can do stuff, and people might still respond badly, but they don't see you being offended by their bad response.

I asked if it was easier not to be seen upset, or for others to see "your reaction to their reaction" as she describes it, and Samantha said, "It's less awkward." In this way, the processing of all this very loud externalization can remain quiet and safe.

The architecture of Facebook and Instagram provides a supportive opportunity to engage in the internal dialogue that can be used to create an emerging, authentic self. Rule #3 creates the path for the reflective work that will be discussed more fully in the final chapter. The space that these sites create via asynchronous communication and integration is grounded in the social rules of the medium's use. Even kids who check feedback constantly can then take the time to reflect upon it later "alone in my room in my pajamas," as one girl described it.

Rule violation

To reiterate, the rules offer a way for teens to confirm visually to themselves and others that they are part of a social group. Symbolic boundaries like these rules are social delineations that help us to understand in-groups and out-groups. As discussed in the introduction, symbolic boundaries can also give people the language and rationale for categorizing the "other" (Lamont 2000). Additionally, and perhaps particularly relevant for adolescents, these symbolic boundaries can be communicated through distinctive physical attributes or props (Goffman 1959), such as dress, to solidify group membership (Blair-Loy 2001). The challenge with boundary work is that while one wants to be distinct from the group so as not to lose one's unique self-concept, one cannot be so distinct that he or she does not appear to fit in with the group (Lamont and Molnar 2002). This tension between standing out and fitting in exists for any group memberships irrespective of age and context (Hewitt 1989); however, it seems likely that this conflict may be exaggerated during adolescence because of the importance of peer groups and social status for this age group. Below is an example of the way that dress communicates group membership for my participant Samantha. In Figure 2.1, which Samantha did not take but was tagged in, the girls are all wearing virtually identical outfits— white shirts and colored skinny jeans, which were very popular with teen girls at the time of my data collection. When speaking to Samantha about this image, she noted that she loved it and thought it was hilarious that so many of her friends were wearing the same outfit to school. For her, this image allows her to see membership in the social group, as their similar outfits serve as a visual confirmation of her peer group membership.

The notion that social belonging matters to teens is certainly not a new concept. Erikson (1980) argues that because adolescents do not have a clear sense of their occupational identity they "temporarily over-identify, to the point of apparent complete loss of identity, with the heroes of cliques and crowds" (97). While this may be an overstatement of the ways symbolic social boundaries create

Figure 2.1 Samantha's Picture of Friends

social hierarchies, his point here is clear: adolescents are aware of how people fit into the groups they would like to join. More interestingly for this work, Erikson 1980) goes on to say that adolescents become "remarkably clannish, intolerant, and cruel in their exclusion of others who are 'different,' in skin color or cultural background, in tastes and gifts, and often in entirely petty aspects of dress and gesture arbitrarily selected as *the* signs of an in-grouper or out-grouper" (97). Adolescents are overly intolerant of others as a way to confirm their own place in the group and solidify social boundaries. Erikson (1980) argues that this behavior is not arbitrary or even mean in its intention, but rather simply a way to manage a lack of a coherent identity. Indeed, he argues that this behavior has some positive consequences: "Adolescents help one another temporarily through such discomfort by forming cliques and by stereotyping themselves, their ideals, and their enemies" (98). For adolescents, this form of intolerance, and the subsequent strengthening of the symbolic boundaries that coincide with it, form very specific categories of worth (Steensland 2006) based on social hierarchies. This can play out on social media via mean or bullying behavior. Thirty-eight percent of participants reported in the survey that someone had been mean to them on social media in the last 12 months, with males reporting higher rates (46 percent) than females

(31 percent). While these numbers may not be as high as some might expect, they indicate that cruelty does happen. Unfortunately, participants made it clear to me in the focus groups that there are some kids who are just more vulnerable to this response. However, the rules play a critical role here; following them ensures that you are not "different," to use Erikson's language. While a picture has to be accurately representative of you, following the rules ensures that the image will not be too different from one's peers.

Teens pay close attention to the rules and those who do not follow them. As a result, those who violate the rules of Facebook are often the targets of mean comments or ridicule. Although the rules are not explained or even discussed in any substantive way until they are violated, these teens have internalized certain social practices about appropriate use of different sites or apps; they know how to use these sites by observing their peers (see Gershon 2010). While none of the girls and only one of the boys in the study violated the social rules of social media that I outlined in this chapter during the observation period, I was able to see others violate the rules occasionally as their pictures came up in my participants' news feeds. What's more, the teens really wanted to talk to me about rule violators. During the focus groups, they seemed to relish the chance to gossip about these people and their posts. For these teens, rule violation is considered a major social faux pas that can have consequences for the violator. Universally, everyone said that the worst thing someone can do is to make overtly cruel or offensive comments. The boys in particular spoke about the danger of sharing religious or political views for fears of being misinterpreted. Racist comments are absolutely taboo, although homophobic slurs, which will be explored in the next chapter, are acceptable and used by both genders, but especially by boys. Beyond cruel and offensive comments, "trying too hard" violates the norms of authenticity. People described as "trying too hard," a term used almost universally by these teens, either try to be something they really are not, or attempt to use social media to fit in with a group of which they are not a part. The images that most frequently received this type of judgment were girls' overtly sexual posing (i.e., trying too hard to appear to be sexy for boys) and party pictures in which people look over-the-top intoxicated (e.g., trying too hard to seem like a cool kid). Overly flattering ("fake") comments on people's pictures, such as "you look like a model" (which many perceive as trying too hard to be accepted by someone/some group through flattery), also received this judgment.

In each of the focus groups, these violations were discussed via examples participants had seen. They seemed to relish the opportunity to talk about the rule violations and violators. This is not surprising given that gossip can serve as a form of social grooming (Dunbar 1998). Framed in this way, gossip provides a way for us to create social cohesion and group delineations. Thus, talking about rule violation is important to teens because it allows them to set and maintain the social boundaries of their group and to confirm that they are comfortably inside those boundaries; that is, it is helpful to talk about what is outside the boundaries of acceptable postings to ensure that yours remain well inside the boundaries.

Embedded in the symbolic boundaries we create are "cultural categories of worth" (Steensland 2006), which we use to judge those who are not part of the in-group. Gossiping about rule violators incorporates these "cultural categories of worth," as it allows participants to assess whether or not they are part of a group and following a group's rules. In the social media world, where teens judge mostly in private, the opportunity to talk openly about the rules with their peers in the focus groups may have provided participants with a chance to engage in this boundary maintenance work and reconfirm their own "categories of worth." This then allows them to formalize their knowledge about what is appropriate on Facebook for their own impression management work.

Perhaps the most interesting example of this boundary work around rule violation took place in one of the focus groups with the older girls. I had asked the girls a few different times during the focus group if they witnessed mean behavior, which they were fairly quick to reject. Then, towards the end of the focus group discussion, Kate mentioned that her senior class has a Facebook page in which people can post or comment. The group then talked about how these class pages generally go; people post things that can be hilarious or annoying, and often include pictures. The conversation, spearheaded by Kate, then turned to a boy who is part of this Facebook group and is known by several members of the focus group from the neighborhood in spite of the fact that the girls do not all go to school together. A full transcription of the discussion about this boy is provided below to give an example of what the group gossip about rule violators can sound like:[1]

Participant:	There are some people on there that do cyber bullying on their [Facebook group] though.
Participant:	Like Peter Antonelli?
Participant:	No, the thing with Peter Antonelli is he like asks for it though.
Many:	He does.
Participant:	*[She turns to the larger group to explain him to the other girls.]* He goes to our school. . . and he makes these statuses. . .
Many:	Oh my God. *[Laughter]*
Participant:	Like once or twice a week and they're just like, I tried to screen-shot them and send it to my friends *[laughs]*, which is kind of mean, but like most of the time I can't, like it won't fit on one thing so I have to do two pictures of them *[laughs]*, and they're literally the most annoying things *[laughs]*. And people are so mean to him on it.
Participant:	No the thing is, he doesn't realize that Facebook is like a joke like you post things that are funny, but he posts serious. . . serious things. *[Laughs]*

Kate then clarified this by reading an excerpt from one of his recent posts about an engineering program jointly offered by MIT and NASA. All the girls laughed throughout her readings. I then asked if he sounds too grown up in the posts, thinking that may be the rule he was violating (i.e., the "poser"), and she said, "The thing about Peter is that he doesn't understand."

Participant:	No he kind of does, it's not like he's mentally unstable or something.
Participant:	No, but he's a bit socially. . .
Many:	Awkward.
Participant:	But it's more like he's being serious. . .
Participant:	He has a girlfriend.
Participant:	He does?
Participant:	He does.
Participant:	And I'm like listening to this like, he has a girlfriend, why does he have a girlfriend, and I don't. . .
Me:	So do people follow relationship statuses?
Participant:	It's really awkward if no one likes your relationship change.
Participant:	But some people like it as a joke, like I liked his relationship change because I thought it was kinda really ironic that he had a girlfriend. So I liked it. [*Laughs*]

This went on for a while, with many more examples of his Facebook faux pas shared. To try to move the conversation forward, I asked if in their opinion this boy was being bullied on social media:

Participant:	A little bit, but he's so oblivious to it. He likes the attention.
Participant:	Like he almost appreciates it. Like he doesn't feel like a victim. He responds to it.
Participant:	Wait, there was this one thing he posted on the group and people were pretty mean about it.
Participant:	That we should wear togas. [*Laughs*]
Participant:	Maybe yeah and then so later he was like, "If anyone has shit to say to me they should say it to my face. I have no respect for people who hide behind their computer screen." Someone says, "Wrestling match, 3rd lunch, the gym" [*all laugh*] and Peter says, "Challenge accepted."
Participant:	See how he says, "Challenge accepted?" He's like. . .
Me:	So he's engaging with them.
Participant:	Right, but like. . .
Participant:	It's kinda sad though because he is, but like. . .
Participant:	It is because he's being serious, but he thinks people are like joking with him to be funny like, being nice to him in a funny way, but really they're just being. . .
Participant:	Being mean to him in a funny way.
Participant:	And other people can see their comments and laugh.
Participant:	Exactly. They're not trying to be funny with him, they're trying to be funny, like about him.
Participant:	This is a real-life example. It's not hypothetical. [*Laughs*]

This conversation illustrates several things about rule violations: First, the sheer enjoyment these girls took in outlining this boy's consistent social missteps on Facebook was evident in their comments. Even when the conversation began to veer into a discussion of relationship status or bullying, Kate immediately brought us back to Peter by reading another one of his posts. They all commented, and while those who did not know the boy were quieter, even they chimed in with judgments when the posts were read. They really felt comfortable assessing him based solely on these posts. Second, there is a clear feeling among these girls that this is not cyber bullying, but rather that this boy brings his problems on himself. Whenever a comment was made that was more sympathetic to Peter and his situation, it was immediately negated by someone else. They claimed that he "likes the attention" and "almost appreciates it. Like he doesn't feel like a victim. He responds to it." There was very little sympathy for Peter, and the group felt that he was entirely to blame for the ridicule he received. Even though they acknowledge that some of the comments directed at him were "mean," they saw them as justified.

Punishment for rule violation is so socially ruthless because of how important these social boundaries are for teens. The rules create the symbolic boundaries, and being a part of the social group, however it is defined by the self, is critical for teens' self-worth and social connectedness. Social belonging is incredibly important for adolescents, as in large part, it is the mechanism through which they feel powerful (Milner 2004). While so much of their lives is dictated by family, school, work, and other responsibilities largely outside of their control, social belonging is earned or lost solely by teens. Social status creates a form of symbolic power as the group accepts the authority of those in high social position (Bourdieu 1984). Adolescents focus on the social hierarchies in which they are embedded because these determine the peer group and romantic options available to them. Social position is not unlimited within the social hierarchy, but rather a finite good that is won or lost. In this conceptualization, if my position improves, it comes at the expense of another group member's status (Milner 2004). As a result, social belonging must be guarded and maintained through markers such as clothes to symbolize inclusion and the "small cruelties" (Milner 2004) that adolescents inflict on one another to ensure their elevated position in the group. So in addition to creating these boundaries, they need to work hard to maintain them, as their position in the social hierarchy relies upon them.

Conclusion

By observing other teens' social media presentations and the reactions they receive on their posts, and via social gossiping about rule violators like Peter Antonelli, these teens have learned the social media rules. It is possible and even likely that teens of other demographics may have different rules than the ones I observed in my study. However, based on data from a few of my participants who have very diverse networks of friends, I believe that while the specific rules may vary, they all perform the same function. The rules are mechanisms through which the teen helps to conceptualize the self as part of a social group. In essence, the rules are part of the self-dialogue.

This, of course, begs the question of how social rules can serve as a tool for self-development when in theory this should be largely individual work. First, social connectedness and belonging are critical components of self-evaluation. This is particularly true in adolescence, when teens are beginning to replace parental approval with peer approval. The rules, then, are important because they ensure that what teens put on social media will be accepted by the group—or not. Although following the rules may sound on the surface to be stressful or negating individuality, the teens I spoke with did not feel this way at all. In fact, they felt that the rules allowed them a great deal of control over their posts. While many spoke of awkward or stressful face-to-face interactions, particularly with romantic interests, all but Jake, the boy who was bullied on Facebook in ninth grade, described presenting the self on social media as relatively safe for them.

The teens talked about the comfort of not having to see someone's reaction, being able to know in advance how images would be received, and having the time and opportunity to choose what images to present for others' judgments. While one could argue that they are hiding behind the screen to avoid messy but important interactions, I think it is also fair to say that social media offers them a chance to control a component of their self-presentation—to think about how the images connect to and tell the story of their emerging self. While everything in our society, including the prosumption component (Davis and Jurgenson 2011) of social media, moves at a frenetic pace, the social media presentation they craft and evaluate later happens at their own time and choosing.

In contrast to those who took comfort in Facebook or Instagram's asynchronous interactions, for Jake, the boy who was bullied on Facebook, the experience was the opposite. He felt more comfortable face-to-face because he just *could not* get the rules; he made several statements in the focus group that were rejected by everyone else as being wrong, and he had the least amount of interaction on his Facebook page of any of my participants. As a result, he did not feel that social media provides visible acknowledgement of his social belonging.

The same is likely to be true for Peter Antonelli, the boy mocked in the girls' focus group. When the girls laughed at Peter Antonelli's rule violations, they did so gleefully. In their view, he was outside of the group and they were comfortably within the boundaries of the group. They did not make the mistakes they observed him making because they knew and followed the rules. Similarly, Jake was more susceptible to rule violation, or perhaps more directly the target of bullying on social media, because he was not part of the group. He violated the rules of trying too hard and being inauthentic, and as a result, he was not able to confirm his place within the boundaries of the social group. I do not suggest that Jake deserved this, but rather note it to indicate how steadfastly these teens police and enforce the rules and how challenging that can be for kids like Jake. Indeed, in his interview, Jake implied that girls had taken screenshots of his messages, the exact thing that Kate did to Peter Antonelli.

This kind of thing does not happen to all kids equally. Thus the rules, while comforting to the majority of these teens who fit within a social group, can be a source of tremendous stress for teens like Jake because they are inextricably tied up with social belonging and the demarcation of group boundaries. While the majority of participants find that social media offers a chance to allow the authentic self to emerge, for teens like Jake it can diminish this opportunity. In effect, the presentation of the personal fable online for some is not a confirmation of the self or a process of moving forward, but a derailment of the developing self.

One last thing to remember: Teens do not *have* to conform rigidly to these rules, and indeed each teen I spoke to adapted them to make them their own. I mentioned earlier how Cassie interprets the rules around a feminine presentation in her own way. So too does Gebre, who described one of his pictures as a "borderline selfie," a taboo for boys to possess, but he notes that he does not care because he likes the picture and what the picture does for him. Marie talked about a girl she knows who will violate the rules to get more likes because social confirmation is important to her. Others, like Noah and Matt, felt no need to worry about the rules, Matt because he already has a girlfriend and Noah because his personal fable emphasizes his rejection of the social media rules and social media "marketing campaign." Yet, as will be evident in the next chapter, while these (and other) teens in the study do violate *some* of the rules, they adhere closely to others. Most of them blend rule observance with rule violation, to interesting effect. For all teens, the rules are a holding pattern that permits entrée into a group.

Note

1 The girls in the focus group were all talking about this boy (whose name has been changed) even if they didn't know him. The result is that it is very hard to determine who was speaking. Rather than guessing or mis-assigning quotes, I have listed the conversation just as "Participant" to indicate a new speaker.

References

Berger, Peter L. and Thomas Luckmann. 1966. *The Social Construction of Reality: A Treatise on the Sociology of Knowledge*. New York, NY: Anchor Books.

Blair-Loy, Mary. 2001. "Cultural Constructions of Family Schemas: The Case of Women Finance Executives" *Gender and Society* 15: 687–709.

Bourdieu, Pierre S. 1984. *Distinction: A Social Critique of the Judgment of Taste*. Translated by Richard Nice. Cambridge, MA: Harvard University Press.

Davis, Jenny. 2012. "Accomplishing Authenticity in a Labor-Exposing Space" *Computers in Human Behavior* 28: 1966–1973.

———. 2013. "Interrogating 'Online' and 'Offline'" *Cyborgology*, edited by Nathan Jurgenson and P. J. Rey. http://thesocietypages.org/cyborgology/2013/08/02/interrogating-online-and-offline/

———. 2014. "Triangulating the Self: Identity Processes in a Connected Era" *Symbolic Interaction* 37: 500–523.

Davis, Jenny and Nathan Jurgenson. 2011. "Prosuming Identity Online" in *Cyborgology*, edited by Nathan Jurgenson and P. J. Rey. http://thesocietypages.org/cyborgology/

Dunbar, Robin. 1998. *Grooming, Gossip, and the Evolution of Language*. Cambridge, MA: Harvard University Press.

Erikson, Erik H. 1980. *Identity and the Life Cycle*. New York: W.W. Norton & Company.

Gershon, Ilana. 2010. *The Breakup 2.0: Disconnecting over New Media*. Ithaca, NY: Cornell University Press.

Goffman, Ervin. 1959. *The Presentation of Self in Everyday Life*. New York, NY: Anchor Books, Doubleday.

Hewitt, John P. 1989. *Dilemmas of the American Self*. Philadelphia, PA: Temple University Press.

Lamont, Michele. 2000. *The Dignity of Working Men: Morality and the Boundaries of Race, Class, and Immigration*. New York, NY: The Russell Sage Foundation.

Lamont, Michele and Virag Molnar. 2002. "The Study of Boundaries in the Social Sciences" *Annual Review of Sociology* 28: 167–195.

Milner, Murray Jr. 2004. *Freaks, Geeks and Cool Kids: American Teenagers, Schools, and the Culture of Consumption*. New York, NY: Routledge.

Steensland, Brian. 2006. "Cultural Categories and the American Welfare State: The Case of Guaranteed Income Policy" *American Journal of Sociology* 111: 1273–1326.

3 The gendered self-narrative

The rules outlined in the previous chapter are universal and in many cases directly mirror offline social norms. Many of these rules, though, are enacted differently by gender, and as such, gender is a powerful narrative documented visually on social media. As Connell and Messerschmidt (2005) write, "Gender is made in schools and neighborhoods through peer group structure, control of social space, dating patterns, homophobic speech, and harassment" (839; see also Thorne 1993). Gender is embedded in all the work teens do and their social spaces and therefore affects both the presentation of other narratives and the enactment of the social rules presented in the previous chapter. For example, developing and articulating emerging political or social values is a narrative arc seen generally in adolescence. Boys in this study reported a willingness to present their beliefs even if they were unpopular with the group, whereas all participants reported that girls are more likely to reiterate the trendy or popular political ideas on social media, suggesting that documenting social belonging visually may be either more relevant for these girls at this moment or that their political stance may be taken less seriously by both males and females. In this case gender impacts what is presented and what is missing from the presentation.

This is important because it means that what these teens are presenting visually are enactments of gendered scripts and roles, particularly those that emphasize masculinity and femininity. This may be surprising given the cultural shifts that have taken place in the twenty-first century; movements in the last few years have challenged traditional ideas around gender and sexual orientation, either via political means (gay marriage, rape trials) or cultural shifts (third-wave feminism, rape culture/consent discussions). However, the emphasis on traditional presentations of masculinity and femininity in adolescence is consistent with the traditional theoretical constructs of gender role development, which point to adolescence as a time in the life course when gender identity is solidified (West and Zimmerman 1987; Gilligan 1982, 1987).

It is important to note, though, that gender is not just something that magically exists; it's not the case that we just *are* a gender. Rather, gender is work. Butler (1990) argues that gender is a "kind of a doing, an incessant activity performed, in part, without one's knowing and without one's willing" (1). Calling upon Goffman's notion of the performance, Butler (1990) writes that gender is not done alone, but rather always performed for others, and like Goffman's dramaturgical approach (1959), there is not one gender performance for each person in all contexts; gender is constructed differently depending on the context. For example, I defined feminine attributes differently when I was in the context of my collegiate rowing team than I did as I prepared for a formal with my roommates. There is no single gender performance, and indeed people employ a variety of different gender strategies that are largely context dependent (Gilligan 1982, 1987; Thorne 1993). Similarly, too, it is important to note that the teens that I interviewed were cisgender, and therefore these findings may not apply to transgender teens. More scholarship is needed in this area.

As social media is a social context in which priority is given to the image, the gender performance there is largely a visual one. This chapter will examine the ways the gender narrative is developed and presented on social media. I argue that the gender narrative is present in the self-preparation work of image creation and curation as well as in the experience of evaluating the image (i.e., the likes, comments, and other forms of feedback) after it has been posted. For comparison, I present the girls' gender norms that I observed and then the boys'. Gendered performances evident in these teens' images create gendered categories of worth around the traditional norms of masculinity for boys and femininity for girls.

Visually depicting femininity

At the outset I think it is worth mentioning that many girls told me that the images could look different depending on the social group they are in (i.e., in some social groups it might be more socially acceptable to post more cleavage shots than in other social groups). They all noted this when they talked about evaluating others' images; that things that they may judge as slutty or trashy may be acceptable in other schools, places, and social groups. I did not see the diversity of imagery they indicated, but I think it is important to present their opinions. Thus, what I show here are the rules that I observed and may not reflect the rules that all girls follow. Nonetheless, I believe that while the images may look different, the overarching themes of the rules will be valid for many girls.

Girls highlight their femininity on social media in two primary ways: via pictures with friends and pictures that emphasize the body and appearance. Images that highlight the body or appearance are fairly straightforward; girls are often dressed in ways that highlight their bodies, which can be as overt as a bikini picture or more subtle. Other images may focus more on the face, often with close-up headshots. With all of these images, the image is crafted in a way that makes it clear that the focus is on the girl's appearance. These are flattering images of the physical self. In friend pictures, which will be discussed below, girls are posed close together, often touching with their arms around each other or hugging. These are usually very posed and often very flattering as well. Sometimes friend pictures will focus more on funny moments between friends. But what is interesting is that for girls the images will always be flattering; a focus on friends will still have everyone looking good; even the silly pictures are not really unflattering. This is in contrast to the boys, who will go out of their way to find embarrassing or unflattering pictures of their friends to post.

Indeed, ensuring that they present the best possible version of the physical self on social media was very important to all of the girls in the study. When I asked Megan about what type of images she sees on social media, Megan told me that a typical girl picture she sees is a photo of a "girl posing with her hand on her waist," again signaling the model style of pose that I often observed in the images. Although, again, they were all clear that they were not trying to look like a model with this pose, but rather they had adopted it because it is very flattering, thereby helping them achieve the best possible version of the self that they want to high-light. I think it is also really important to note that almost all of the comments girls received, regardless of the type of image, focused on appearance. While this may not be as common for sports images (which were rarely posted by girls in the study), almost all the other pictures received comments about the appearance of the girl or girls in the picture. One of the participants in particular told me that, even with pictures of close friends, the comments will often be focused on the girls' appearance. So even in pictures that are intended to highlight friendship, the comments will often be "you're so pretty" instead of anything about the girls' friendship.

Documenting relationships matters to girls. Images with friends in close embrace, being silly, or even posing as models are all over their news feeds. While social belonging is an important piece of the personal fable narrative in adolescence, many scholars have argued that this is especially true for girls. With her concept of "self in relation," Surrey (1980) argued that women evaluate the self within the context of their relationships, and thus "the primary experience of the self [for women] is relational" (2). In this way, the self is always regarded "in the context of important relationships" (2). This relational theory of the self is sup-ported by Gilligan (1982) and Miller (1976), among others, and it would explain why relationships play such an important role in girls' social media visual fables. If relationships factor heavily into girls' narrative of self, they will be prominently displayed in the social media visual. When asked to describe the types of pic-tures she typically sees, Kate, an 18-year-old girl, told me that the "standard girl's picture is a group of girls with their arms around each other smiling." Every girl has this picture. She went on to say that this type of image is important because it shows "these are my friends." This is a perfect articulation of Surrey's (1980) "self in relation" concept; Kate describes this picture as visually showing the self in the context of peer relationships, and notes that it is really important for girls to have this to show. Being a good friend, or perhaps, for this visual context, being seen by others and the self as one who has many friends, is very important to girls' self-conception.

Image creation: enlist your friends to create the fable

In addition to showing friendships and giving off the impression (Goffman 1959) of being a good friend, girls' relationships play a role in the image creation pro-cess as well. In the previous chapter, I mentioned that girls do not talk about their day-to-day social media experiences with their friends. However, unlike boys, girls reported that they enlisted their friends to help create the visual narrative.

They consulted with their friends about what images to post and whether to use an image as a timeline, cover, or profile picture, and they relied on friends to suggest the most flattering or best picture possible. The younger girls even coordinated photo shoots that involved friends discussing everything from wardrobe choices to poses to backgrounds.

Photo shoots demonstrate how attractiveness and social belonging come together for a feminine presentation of the self. The girls talked about setting up photo shoots where they coordinate with their friends to take pictures with the express purpose of putting them on social media. They are designed to ensure that clothing, hair, makeup, and pose are as flattering as possible. One of the 18-year-old girls said that there is a difference between what she called "planned and natural clothes" for the photo shoots. What she meant by this is that there are times when girls will select clothes for photo shoots (i.e., the "planned" clothes) that are often more dressed up and very flattering (an example of this style of image might be a girl posed in a dress with her hair and makeup done and posing in her backyard). In contrast, there are pictures that girls take of friends in which they are wearing more casual clothes (i.e., the "natural" clothes) that they probably wore that day. These images might show a girl posed in the yard in her jeans and a sweater, for example. It will still be a flattering image, but the image may feel more natural and less crafted. Amala, a chatty ninth-grade girl who is not allowed to have Facebook, but who actively participates in many photo shoots for her friends' Facebook, described the process for me: "No like um, my friends and I, well one of my friends has, her backyard has like really nice lighting. . . And so when one of them needs like a new pro pic,[1] we'll, we'll actually like go in there and. . . look nice and we'll take pictures." Amala said that they help each other select clothes, suggest poses for the picture, and then evaluate the options to select the best one for posting. Photo shoots offer girls the chance to show their attractiveness, but the resulting picture in which they tag friends who were there with "photo creds"[2] also indicates something about their social capital via friendships and social connectedness. It is a collaborative process that marks both their attractiveness and group membership.

Figure 3.1 shows ninth-grader Izzy's photo shoot with friends. It was taken in a context similar to the one described by Amala. Her image is stylized and is markedly different from her other social media pictures in terms of pose and her use of Instagram filters. When I asked Izzy to describe this image, she said that her good friend took the picture while they were "goofing around" in the yard being "arty." This term, "arty," came up often with the girls as a way to describe images that appear to be influenced by stylized fashion magazine editorial spreads (Mears 2011). When asked about these types of images, the girls referred to these poses as "model posing." In these images, more care is given to the background, lighting, clothing, and pose than in the girls' other photographs. They may often use a filter for these images as well. They based a lot of the arty label on the pose, which, like Izzy's pose in Figure 3.1, is less standard and often involved the girl looking away from the camera. In Kate's version of an "arty" picture, she and a friend are posed on a stone wall, their backs to each other, staring straight ahead; the image

Figure 3.1   Izzy's "Arty" Profile Picture

was taken of them in profile. I think, too, that the term "arty" also gives these girls some protection from the feedback and rules; if the image is described as arty, it implies that they were doing it to be artistic, not trying too hard to look good.

To understand the differences between the photo shoot images and equally important but less stylized photos, Figures 3.2 and 3.3 show two of ninth-grader Cassie's images. The first (Figure 3.2) is clearly staged, and could be described as an "arty" picture from a photo shoot. While the other (Figure 3.3) was still posed and edited through Instagram, it was described to me as a "typical teen selfie." (I think by this they mean natural and not obviously staged.) The second image was taken by the girl on the left, and although it is flattering in its way, is not overly "done" or staged.

Cassie told me that she feels ambivalent about photo shoots. In the following exchange, she gently mocks those who spend hours doing photo shoots while also acknowledging the value of the end product: "I mean people go out and they're like, 'Alright today I'm gonna make a new profile picture' . . . And spend like three hours like going around like taking artsy pictures. Then obviously when you're posting it, you don't just want to be like, 'Okay I want like my three best friends to see this.' You want to be like, 'I want a good [picture], I'm proud of this

Figure 3.2 Cassie's Photo Shoot Image

Figure 3.3 Cassie's "Typical Teen Selfie"

picture and I want like a good portion of people, I mean guys, too, to see this." '
Cassie subtly mocks the girls who spend three hours taking "artsy" pictures and
also is quick to note that it is her friends, not her, who will initiate the photo shoot;
however, at the same time she also says that it is "nice to get a really good picture
of yourself." And once she gets this great picture of herself, it is important to her
that others, particularly boys, see it.

I will discuss Cassie's example again in the next chapter, but the important
thing to note here about photo shoots is that Cassie suggests that she likes seeing
the image, too. While we can lament the fact that girls worry about appearance
to the extent that they do, I argue that this is not a new experience, with one key
exception. The photo shoots give the girls such control over image creation that
almost everyone finds a good picture. Even Cassie, who says that she often does
not end up with a profile picture, still has that positive feeling of seeing a "good
picture" of herself. Although my data cannot prove a correlation, there is reason
to question whether this experience of seeing the self in what she deems to be a
flattering image on social media can positively affect self-esteem.

Additionally, it is important to note that while they may be doing model poses
or photo shoots, none of the girls spoke about trying to reach some unattainable
popular culture definition of beautiful. Because of the value these adolescents
placed on authenticity, they indicated to me that the goal is not to look like a
model, but rather to present, as Amala said, "your best self. . . Like *you* look
good." Many girls reiterated the point of showcasing your "best self." While they
all said that profile pictures present the most flattering image available, it still has
to look like you. While almost every girl had some sort of bathing suit or bikini
shot, a variety of body types were shown. None of the girls in my study were
significantly overweight, and as such, my results may be skewed, but still it is
important to note that the stress was not about looking super thin or model beautiful, but about appearing as your best self.

While the older girls do not engage in photo shoots as often as the younger
girls, friends still play an important role in image creation. In the first chapter
I presented Marie's description of selecting a prom picture based on her sister's
approval. First her sister was planning to post her own prom picture, which gave
Marie the idea to look for a picture, too. Then Marie asked her sister which of the
pictures she liked best, at which point Marie "just like decided to do that one."
Only after she received approval did Marie say, "I felt like that was like the best
one." Marie makes it clear that, while her sister's isn't "the only opinion in the
world," she relies on her for help with image selection. Finally, she implies that
Lucy, her sister, gives her reassurance that the selected image does not violate the
rules—in her words, it's not "weird, too." Although the picture is an individual
shot of Marie in her dress for prom, the image curation process is all about her
relationship with her sister, who happens to be a good friend.

Marie's example again illustrates the link between social belonging (i.e., self
in relation theory [Surrey 1980]) and appearance. Marie is a harsh judge of her
appearance, and having her sister tell her that it was a good picture (and in the
girls' vernacular a critical component of a "good" picture is that it is flattering) led

her to see the image in a more positive light. While feedback generally comes in the form of likes after the image is posted, in some ways Marie got her feedback and began the meaning-making process with her sister's approval in this preparation phase, before the image was even posted. Because of this type of pre-posting feedback, it is not surprising that girls do not spend much time discussing the image after it is posted; they already know what people will think, and in a sense, the initial self-evaluative work sets the frame for the individual work that they do.

Sexualized femininity in the presentation of the self

In addition to flattering images that highlight the face, the body is an important component of appearance in girls' images. Indeed, these are often inextricably linked. As is evident in some of the earlier photo shoot images, girls also present the feminine self via sexualized images. These images were varied, but often involved overly posed shots that highlight cleavage or the body more generally. The posed bikini shots in particular are a good example of this. I saw a lot of these images during the observation period; indeed, almost every girl had these sexualized appearance-driven images. Although only one of my focus groups with girls was conducted during the summer (i.e., "bikini season"), twelve of the thirteen girls had bikini pictures posted on the timelines, but never as their profile pictures. It is worth it to pause here and describe these images because they were so prevalent in the girls' images. While there are variations on the bikini pictures, there were some clear visual themes in these images. Bikini pictures can be taken anywhere; often they are outside on the beach, by the pool, or in a field, yard, or on a deck. These pictures were often deemed "natural" as they were taken in an outdoor location. However, sometimes bikini pictures are taken inside; girls in the study had posed bikini pictures indoors and mirror selfie bikini pictures (often with friends, who are also wearing bikinis). The full body bikini images often include some aspects of the model posing such as the hands on hips pose, and many of the bikini pictures also include friends. One interesting bikini picture was posted in the winter with the caption "miss summer." To be sure, the younger girls (13–14) had fewer images that highlighted the body in a sexual way, and the tone of their bikini pictures, like Melissa's image (Figure 3.4), is more subtle than the older girls' bikini images.

As part of the interviews with the girls, I showed them two bikini images that were posted by girls unknown to them. Because bikini images were so prevalent in the study, I wanted to understand how girls read these images and also if and how they judge other females' images. This was particularly important because, despite the frequency with which I observed bikini pictures, they were often referenced by boys and girls in the focus groups in a judgmental way. The faces were blurred to ensure anonymity, so admittedly they could not assess facial expressions clearly. The two images were selected as representations of the two typical styles of bikini pictures I observed online; one showed two girls arm in arm, both wearing bikinis and posed on what looks like a deck. There are palm trees in the background, but the girls are standing on a wood floor. When I asked the girls

Figure 3.4 Melissa's Version of a Bikini Picture

to guess which of the two girls in the image had posted it to social media, every girl in the study correctly guessed the poster. When I asked them how they could assess this, they all responded that she just "looks better" in the image.

The second image shows a girl in a bikini top and frayed jean shorts standing in a parking lot. She may or may not have been at the beach, we cannot tell from the angle of the shot. Her head is tilted slightly to the left and she is waving at the camera. This image was evaluated by many girls as "trying too hard" because it was taken outside of a beach context; the palm trees in the background of the other picture was highlighted to contrast these images. A few girls did think it was less posed and said the fact that she is waving made it feel more awkward and less strategic.

The prevalence of bikini pictures makes an interesting statement about how these girls view femininity. The survey data indicates that these girls are well rounded; according to their survey responses, 54 percent of the girls played on two or more sports teams during the previous year, and many spoke in their interviews about involvement in extracurricular activities. Yet comparatively, very few of their images highlighted these activities on Facebook. While these pictures are there, they are not posted nearly as often as the body/image pictures. The question then becomes, what this might say about what girls want or need to highlight? Is it that the physical self must be on display more frequently? Or alternatively, thinking of the self-evaluative work, is the physical self what they really seek feedback on from their social media audiences? It is outside the scope of my research to determine the cause of this, but I believe it is important to ask these questions.

The girls receive a lot of feedback for these images, and they seem to enable some girls to reject the universal rules described in the previous chapter; some of these very sexualized body image shots challenge the norms of authenticity and "trying too hard." But it was clear in my conversations with the girls that these body images receive a lot of likes; girls' friends like flattering pictures, and boys may like these as well. If social media gender performances mirror, albeit in an amplified way, traditional norms, it is plausible to assume that there is an "erotic market" on social media that functions in a way similar to those Hamilton (2007) and Armstrong, Hamilton, and Sweeney (2006) documented on college campuses. Their research, along with Bogle's (2008) work on the gendered standards of the "hookup culture," suggests that females may use feminine and erotic gendered performances to enhance their social status amongst peers (Hamilton 2007; Armstrong et al. 2006). Given the circular logic of social media, these likes signal to the girl that she looks good. Thus, she can enact a feminine and sexualized role for the picture that emphasizes appearance in order to receive confirmation that she is in fact pretty and feminine and perhaps enhance her status with her peers. Again, the self in relation (Surrey 1980) and appearance intersect here. Although it is beyond the scope of this research, it would be interesting to examine the long-term effect on adolescent girls of visually producing the gendered role.

Experiencing the image: likes in relation

Even after they have posted an image, the process is still relational for girls as they begin to receive likes and comments. While peer help selecting and curating images gives them a sense before the post of how many likes they will receive, the girls were unabashed in their quest for likes. If girls are operating on a "self in relation" (Surrey 1980) trajectory of development, then likes are important for them because they provide visual evidence of girls' social belonging on some level. They may giggle about some of the methods they use to "up their likes" and talk snidely about girls who use these techniques a bit too often and obviously, but they all have a long list of strategies that they feel comfortable using to get more likes. Again, because of the importance of presenting an authentic self, they have to be a bit discreet about it and cannot pursue all of these like strategies at once, but they are all at their disposal. This is a perfect example of the Goffman (1959) notion of impression given versus given off. The crucial thing here is that the work that they do to "up their likes" cannot give off the impression of trying too hard. Rather, it must appear to be subtle and give off an impression of authenticity. Table 3.1 outlines the most commonly referenced like strategies girls I interviewed either employed themselves or saw other girls utilize. The girls noted that

Table 3.1 Girls' Strategies to Increase Likes

Strategy	Mechanism
Initial Posting Strategies	
Reciprocal Likes	Like other people's pictures so they feel "obligated to like yours back."
Choose Photomates Wisely	Taking pictures with "high likes"[3] people will get you more likes.
Aim for Peak Visibility	Post your images during peak Facebook times (weeknights 7 p.m.—12 a.m.) in order to maximize the number of friends who will see it within the critical window.
Enlist Friends	Most girls said that they felt obligated to like and/or comment on their close friends' pictures. Girls might let a close friend know that they posted a new picture to ensure that they get some early likes.
Strategies for Increasing Likes After the Critical Five-Hour Window Has Passed	
Tag Yourself	Several days/weeks (although they said three days was the average) after the image was posted they can tag themselves in their own picture. This serves no purpose other than to resurface the image in the news feed for visibility.
Repost Pictures	Repost a picture so that it resurfaces in the news feed.
Reply to Comments	The image will likely generate a few comments. If they wait to respond to the comments, the picture will again resurface in the news feed.

you generally have a five-hour window in which your image will be seen before it descends too far down the news feed and loses visibility. After the five-hour window, they begin using the second set of strategies to try to "up their likes" and bring their post up higher in the news feed.

The extensive work that girls do to ensure likes may feel inauthentic to us; if they are strategizing so aggressively for likes, it cannot really present their true selves. But what is interesting is that the girls described something potentially empowering in these strategies. The girls told me that taking these actions gives them some degree of control over their feedback; utilizing these strategies means that girls do not have to wait to see how their pictures "do" (their word for the number of likes they receive), but rather it gives them some control over promoting their pictures. It was interesting to hear them talk about these strategies, as it was clear the girls believed they really work. While they can giggle about them in conversation with an adult, I cannot help but think these strategies, while overwhelmingly time-consuming, do in fact give them some control over the outcome, despite the prosumption (Davis and Jurgenson 2011) aspect of social media that gives others the ability to create content on your social media. And perhaps in some ways, they may be able to use these strategies to react against the prosumptive nature of social media? If they must produce something that is consumed and then added to and assessed online, these strategies give them an opportunity to control, at least in small part, how much or how little their content is seen and responded to by their peers. They can choose how much effort to put into getting likes, and while they cannot manufacture likes for themselves, they can at least increase their chances.

Experiencing the image: indirect meanness

Echoing gender norms that emphasize niceness in girls, I observed no incidents of direct meanness in the girls' interactions on Facebook during the observation period. But in talking with them in the interviews and focus groups, it became clear that they are mean; they just engage in subtle, indirect meanness that would easily be missed by outside observers. The subtly cruel behavior that teen girls engage in is well documented in the literature (e.g., Wiseman 2002), and therefore it is no surprise that it has found a home on social media, too. Girls reported that it is common to crop other girls out of pictures or purposely not like or comment on certain girls' postings, which is no small slight given the reciprocity norms that girls have regarding likes. Tagging can also be used to slight people; while the teens often said they will not tag people in a picture if they are not social media friends with them, a few indicated that tagging can be a way to create boundaries between people. One girl said that she will tag her close friends and then "I just kind of get tired and stop," which indicates a hierarchy of friendships. One girl was on the receiving end of this, telling me about an example where she was not tagged in a group picture when "everyone else was." Girls similarly talked about feeling sad when they were excluded from a social event documented on social media. One 18-year-old girl spoke at length about seeing a picture on social media of "all of [her] friends hanging out" and realized she was not included in the gathering. Despite the fact that many had experiences like this themselves, and almost everyone knew of someone who had, the girls were unanimous in their assertions that they would not discuss these slights with their friends. None of them could think of an example where a girl had confronted another girl to ask why she was excluded or edited out of a picture. So the online indirect meanness is never discussed among these teen girls.

Girls also judge other girls' posts harshly, especially when it comes to bikini shots that emphasize the body. These images especially are risky because they can easily send the wrong impression of trying too hard. There was some disagreement among the girls about what actually constitutes trying too hard with bikini shots. As mentioned in an earlier section, I showed two bikini pictures to the girls in the interviews to get a sense of how they would speak about an image they had not posted or from a person they do not know. In the picture with the two girls in bikinis posed arm in arm, they are both doing the hands on hip pose, and one girl has her knee bent as well, part of the "model pose" mentioned earlier. The girls' opinions about this image were mixed; some described it as "forced" and "annoying," given that the girls in the picture are not actually at the beach and therefore just "wanted to have a picture to show." Other girls said it was an acceptable vacation picture because there are "palm trees in the back," so they could actually have been heading out or coming from the beach. As one girl said, "So I think the fact that they're sort of being like casual like their arms around each other, it just seems more like friends on the beach rather than like trying to you know get attention." For the other picture, with the girl in a bikini top and jean shorts waving at the camera from a parking lot, many found this to be annoying or trying too hard, although similarly the reaction to this image was mixed as well. After a negative evaluation of the image as "just kinda like screams to get your attention," one 18-year-old girl said, "I mean still she could be a nice person." It is clear that girls read motives into images based on pose, clothing, attractiveness, and environment, even with girls they have not met.

And this is not necessarily a bad thing. Dunbar's (1998) seminal work on the power and importance of gossip for social cohesion suggests that judgment and gossip can be helpful, as we use them to delineate appropriate behavior and boundaries, something that these girls are clearly doing when they read these images. And importantly, while I think it is important to document their readings of the images and the girls in the images, I do not judge them for judging. What is important for this work is that they believe that they *can* read images correctly. While they may disagree with each other, none of the girls were confused or muddled in their assessments.

Girls can also be mean by using social media and cell phone technology to spread gossip or make fun of people via relational aggression (Crick and Grotpeter, 1995). Girls can take screenshots of social media interactions to share with others at a later date. In the previous chapter, I gave the example of Kate's screenshots of Peter's posts in their class group, which she shared with the focus group. Jake, the boy in the study who had been a victim of Facebook bullying in the ninth grade, mentioned that he is concerned about girls taking screenshots of his posts because it has happened to him in the past. Jake said he finds it to be challenging to approach girls on social media because "like if someone just like takes a crack at someone like, like the girl like screenshots the photo and like sends it to her guy friends. . . Like so many times." He went on to describe screenshotting as:

> That's the worst, that's the worst part. . . You know like, if like, if a girl isn't into me like after I go up to her or something like that it's like, "Oh okay, whatever" . . . Whereas like, if I was like, if I like message a girl that I saw at a party, never even talked to and I was like, "Hey do you remember me?" or something like [in] a position of weakness. And then it's just like, don't respond, shows that they read it, screenshot it, like send it to a bunch of her girlfriends. . . Or whatever you get seen as like a loser of some sort of, something like that. So I wouldn't put myself in that position in the first place.

Jake implies he would never approach a girl on Facebook because it puts you in "a position of weakness" where she can take your words and then share them with everyone to make you look like "a loser of some sort." Girls' use of technology to engage in gossiping and relational aggression (Crick and Grotpeter 1995) was particularly upsetting to Jake, and he labeled it "mean-spirited." His word choice implies a power dynamic at play; girls seem to be able to wield this technique to gain the position of power.

Naturally, though, this power play is connected to the symbolic boundaries and the categories of social worth described in the previous chapter. The individual or group has the power to cut out others; however, girls would never screenshot a high-status boy's message. Rather, it is someone like Jake, who has struggled on Facebook in the past, who becomes the victim of the boundary work. The boundaries are dynamic and therefore often ambiguous, which means that feelings can be hurt. While this can certainly happen to boys and girls (I will highlight examples of boys' meanness in the next section), the point of difference I observed is that when the girls are being "mean-spirited," it is never overt (Wiseman 2002; Crick and Grotpeter 1995). Rather, they engage in subtle meanness and relational aggression to signal group boundaries without actually saying anything that could be categorized as cruel by an outside observer. Boys are more obviously mean, which creates interactions and dialogues around meanness. The girls' actions, on the other hand, are harder to address. In all of the interviews, girls said that they never say anything when they are excluded or hurt by friends on Facebook. As Kate said,

> I don't know. I feel like if you feel bad about it you're probably not going to talk about it. But, yeah, I don't know. Like yeah, I don't know. It can happen like if you weren't invited to a party and you see a ton of pictures and just like that feels bad, but I can't remember any specific time.

The subtle seems hard to call out, and as a result, the internalization process happens largely alone.

Status trumps the rules

In the focus group conversations, it was very clear that girls allow certain high-status people more leeway in following the rules. While the boys militantly enforce the rules and call out any violator, the girls make it pretty clear that high-status girls can violate the rules without facing the same types of negative consequences that lower-status girls would face; in this way, status confers privilege to violate the rules. While the norms around subtle meanness do hold for most girls, many acknowledged that higher-status people do not have to be as subtle. One of the girls in the focus group said that "the popular people post more and can be more aggressive. . . mean to other kids" than less high-status kids. Similarly, during a focus group conversation about the likes strategies mentioned above, someone shared the example of a popular girl known to many, who ruthlessly employs most, if not all, of the strategies each time she posts a picture. For most girls, the impression this would send is of being inauthentic and trying too hard, which are some of the biggest social violations on social media. Yet because of this girl's high status, she faced no significant consequences for breaking the rules. They all noticed it and mentioned that it was "annoying" because, as one girl put it, "especially because she's a person that already has so many [likes], it's like why do you have to do that?" But in spite of this annoyance, they acknowledged that they will like her posts and that there are no negative social consequences for her violation of the rules. This is in direct contrast to Jake, who had to shut down his Facebook in ninth grade because he was bullied for "trying too hard" to be popular, the exact behavior in which this popular girl engages. While I think there is an important gender difference in the way that meanness plays out on social media, I do think there is also something about the importance of the social hierarchy for girls. The girls made it clear that the freedoms certain girls are allowed does not apply to lower-status girls, which implies to me that the Facebook rules are more strictly adhered to by lower-status girls because of the social categories of worth that exist.

Boys' rules: be real, masculine, and stupid funny

In my analysis, I was able to decode fewer gendered rules for boys, and indeed boys' images in the observation period were more varied than girls, who tended to produce lots of images that replicated their friends' pictures and/or ones they had previously posted. But in spite of fewer specific rules, masculinity norms were all-pervasive, usurping all the rules mentioned in the previous chapter for adolescent boys. More than 30 years ago, Pleck (1981) noted an important homosexual/heterosexual dichotomy inherent in adolescent male peer relationships, whereby boys compete with and compare themselves to other boys based on how "manly" they are. To negotiate this competition, Kimmel (1994) writes that in adolescence male peers serve as a "kind of gender police, constantly threatening to unmask us as feminine" (148). Indeed, Connell's (1995) notion of a "hegemonic masculinity" exhibited in adolescent males appears to be as firmly embedded in the teen social structure today as it was 20 years ago. Although the term has come under criticism in recent years, Connell and Messerschmidt (2005) defend the concept, noting that there is a "hierarchy of masculinities" (831) in an "active struggle for dominance" (832), with hypermasculine men at the top of the hierarchy. Of course, while the concept of what is considered most dominant can evolve over time, the notion of a competitive hierarchy will remain. Connell and Messerschmidt (2005) note that there may not be many men who can actually achieve the top position in any given social group, however it "was certainly normative. It embodied the currently most honored way of being a man, it required all other men to position themselves in relation to it . . . " (832). This ideal version of masculinity is what males use to judge their own gendered worth and position. This work, of comparing the self to the ideal, is what I heard the boys in the study talk about most often. When they say things are "what guys do" or "that's not manly," they are in essence evaluating themselves based on this hierarchy. The interesting component here is that they have to do the masculine presentation visually.

Yet it is reductive to assume on social media that traditional gender norms are just being enacted on a different platform. Something is new here because the technological features require males to be on display in visual images in a way that has hitherto not been a large part of the teenage male experience. I asked the boys about the image they were trying to create on social media, and the majority said that they just wanted to come across as "normal" kids. Peter said that now that he is headed to college and future classmates will be looking at his social media before meeting him in person, he has started to think about the type of first impression a stranger might get from his Facebook: "And I started thinking about that, I was like. . . like I wonder what my profile looks like from like an outsider [perspective]." When I asked if he had any ideas, he laughed and said, "I don't know, I hoped I was just a normal kid."

Matt said that his only goal is "not trying to make myself [look like] an idiot." These goals—just looking "normal" or trying not to look like "an idiot"—sound really banal and obvious; of course we all want that! However, after examining their images and talking to the boys about their pictures, it was clear that looking "normal" is their coded language for wanting to look authentically masculine, which is conveyed via the standard boy attributes—pictures of sports and girls, and images where they appear comfortable looking funny or idiotic from time to time. The "normal" boy that participants speak about is a masculine boy. As with girls, all of these attributes are projected through the surface self-presentation and lead boys to enact heteronormative gender scripts. They work hard to adhere to this, but largely disguise their efforts, as they reported that trying too hard and caring about how you look are feminine behaviors. This concept will be explored later, but for now, it is important to note that many of the boys told me that "there's an idea of like boys are not like supposed to worry about their appearance or something like that." Again, based on Connell and Messerschmidt's (2005) notion that the "plurality of masculinities" are in an "active struggle for dominance" (232), the boys are clear that the ideal version of masculinity would involve not caring about how they look. As a result, many said that selfies are "taboo." When I asked why selfies were not allowed, I received several answers that are variations on the same theme: "Cause then it's like, then you're trying to, like you're worrying about your appearance and how people see it." Or the idea that selfies are only okay if you take one with a girl because "the girl's in it and girls take pictures of everything." Yet, while they need to adhere to these gender norms, all but one boy, Noah (who I discuss in greater depth in Chapters 1 and 4), said that they want to look good and have flattering pictures to post on social media. This is a challenge to the ideals of masculinity that they articulate. Connell and Messerschmidt (2005) would not see this as a problem, noting that very few males can or do adhere to the ideal. I think this is important to establish here to understand more fully how these boys negotiate the masculine presentation; they are trying to find flattering images for social media and also adhere to the ideal norms of masculinity that suggest that appearance and caring about appearance should not matter.

The creation and curation of the masculine self

Gendered norms are pervasive in the production and display of boys' images, which highlight their most masculine activities, usually sports, even if boys have multiple interests. In many ways, this is no different from the well-rounded girls who focus on their bodies in their images. Charlie, a senior in the study, talked about how he was very involved in Irish dancing in his hometown, which he never shared with his classmates for fear of ridicule. As Charlie describes, "So for a while up until my sophomore year I um, did some competitive Irish step dancing. . . So it's a weird story, so I, but I didn't tell anyone at Pierce about it. It's sort of like my little secret." To maintain this secret on social media, Charlie used the untag feature on Facebook to ensure that dance pictures did not surface on his news feed. He laughed and explained,

> I was very sure to keep everything kosher you know, no crossover because you know I didn't, you know I was kind of shy about it. . . I would like find a way to subtly untag myself in every single like photo from Irish dancing.

I asked him why he did this, and he first explained that the dance group was part of a "really bizarre subculture" that his school friends would not understand. But after talking it through for a minute, he said, "But I think at first it was an element of embarrassment." I asked if any of his dance friends noticed that he was untagging himself, and he said they did see it and some "were offended but I think they more or less understood, 'Okay you know you're a guy who goes to an all-guys school, probably don't want to [share this with them].'"

Charlie implies that he worries that his friends will view his Irish step dancing as unmanly. He used the Facebook technology of untagging to distance himself and thereby control his image. His Irish dance friends can still see the images other people post; however, by untagging himself from these images, he ensures that his male school friends will not see them. Thus, the same tool that makes the embarrassing photos visible in the first place can be used to limit their damage to one's sense of self. Charlie did not feel that this was inauthentic, and I tend to agree with him; Goffman (1959) would argue that gearing one's performance, in this case through images, to the perceived audience is what we all do in our everyday lives. The fact that the performance is more permanent because of its visual nature on social media does not mean it is any less authentic than what happens offline.

Charlie mentioned that a friend does a similar thing with his theater pictures:

> I have a friend who, he's an awesome squash player. And he is really into theater. And he has, you know, for every, excuse me, one theater picture, he'll have like a hundred squash pictures. Even though [theater is] a big part of his life. And if you talk to him in person, he wouldn't be ashamed of that at all but I think online he would.

Charlie notes that this boy will talk about his love of theater in person, but will minimize the space he gives theater on his Facebook page. Charlie says that he would be "ashamed" to have his theater interests highlighted on Facebook, which indicates the power of the masculine presentation of the self. Charlie (and perhaps his friend) seem to think that the presentation online should be more manly, to use their language, than it needs to be in person. I think this is because of the power of the visual; perhaps it feels more important to have the visual image match up to an ideal as that becomes a visual and, in the case of the profile picture, more lasting first impression. I think it is also worth noting that it's not just sports that can highlight the ideal masculinity, although that was certainly the most common way that I observed. There were also a few teen boys in the study who played instruments, and they posted their music pictures on social media. Although, interestingly, as in evidence in Figure 3.5, it was mostly boys who played guitar and were dressed in a way that suggests they play rock music (or at least not chamber music!). Charlie also notes that it is his understanding that this is common practice for all boys.

While Charlie talks about his friend's postings, all of the boys were adamant that they do not discuss their posts with their friends, as that is another behavior labeled as feminine. Indeed, there were many things that the boys told me were feminine images and behaviors that they had to work to avoid in their curation and presentation of images. Below is a list of the actions that were described to me as "girly" or "something only girls do" by the boys. These examples will be discussed more fully in the text, but for now the goal is just to provide an overall sense of the types of things they consider feminine, and therefore off limits, on social media.

Image Creation:

- Setting up photo shoots
- Constantly taking pictures
- Ensuring a flattering picture by looking at the image and asking the photographer to take more
- Overt posing or selfies
- Discussing the image or posting the image at the time of creation

Image Curation:

- Any type of editing of the image, with the exception of cropping or additions that add humor (text, etc)
- Discussing which picture to post with friends
- Asking friends to like images

Social Media Behaviors:

- Liking a lot of images
- Appearing to care a lot about how many likes you receive
- Posting a lot of images

But here is the challenging part: while they have to avoid as many of the feminine behaviors as possible, they have to navigate them to some degree; it is hard to have something to put on social media without taking pictures. Indeed I would argue that social media requires boys to engage with these taboo feminine behaviors simply to be able to have something to post. As mentioned earlier, boys rely

Figure 3.5 Charlie's Guitar Timeline Picture

on their parents to take pictures for them to ensure that they are not called out as "not manly" for requesting photos at special events. Gebre described the strategies he sees boys employ, which, although they do not contain the peer support component embedded in Amala's experience, virtually mimic what she described the girls doing in their photo shoots. Gebre talked about another strategy, photobombing, that boys can employ to get the pictures that they want:

> Yes. One hundred percent yeah I think people are always um, aware of them and always looking for like they're always like, they're always um, constantly like thinking about like, I think probably when like if they see an opportunity to like get a picture without having to ask for a picture or something like that they'll try. And get it, yeah you see it, it's kind of like animals like you go to a party. . . You see one person like taking pictures people always like, guys especially you like are always like running into like the picture like photobombing. Just to get into it. And like, 'cause they want, you know they want that photo to be able to post it. Without having to ask for the picture or take a picture themselves.

He said that this behavior is obvious, but noted that "people try to like be discreet about it. . . Or people try to act like they don't, they don't care." Getting a picture for social media can lead boys to strategies like photobombing because "they want that photo to be able to post it" on social media. These boys are clearly engaged in the fan dance (Jurgenson and Rey 2013) between the reveal and conceal here; by appearing to just jump into a picture as a spur-of-the-moment decision, these boys are concealing the very strategic work involved in getting an image that they want. After all, they are not photobombing just to be in the picture; they are photobombing because they want to have *that* picture to post on social media. While their images do not appear as stylized as the girls', they are investing a significant amount of effort in their social media presentation. Considering social media and the images you want, while also managing your face-to-face interactions at a party, is a lot for teens to negotiate. That they bother at all suggests that the images hold a great deal of meaning for them. It allows them to signal with an image "look at this great thing and by the way I look good" all while concealing a great deal of their feminine work to create the image.

The masculine preparation work: authenticity as a masculine strategy

In Chapter 2, I presented authenticity as an overarching Facebook rule, basically the idea that you have to be yourself, or the "best version" of yourself, but you cannot be fake. Authenticity is worth highlighting here because of how boys utilize authenticity as a means of downplaying the self in preparation work that they do on Facebook. By overemphasizing how authentic they are in the presentation of the self, boys can actually downplay all their work to get good pictures that highlight the right aspect of their personal fable. Additionally, downplaying their work serves the dual purpose of confirming their position in the masculinity hierarchy, as the work is deemed feminine. It is interesting to me that authenticity can be used to confirm a masculine performance and vice versa.

Noah described himself as having no agenda or strategy on Facebook because he just showed his true self on Facebook. When asked if he thought about how he would be perceived by others, he said, "I don't really care that much." He cares very much about giving off the impression of authenticity and takes pride in his antisocial tendencies. His pictures do have a different look and feel from the majority of the boys and tend to be less focused on presenting a typically flattering image of the self. In many of the images, like the one in Figure 3.6, he makes goofy or funny faces in the picture on purpose.

However, at the same time, given the images he selected, the posing he did, and the language he used in the interview, it is clear that he was working hard to create his narrative. That narrative just happened to be the story of someone who could care less. Additionally, he was very aware that when pictures are taken they will end up on social media, saying, "Like whenever someone takes a picture, it's probably gonna end up on Facebook." Despite all of this, he was still presenting a masculine self; he was often pictured with girls who gave off (Goffman 1959) the impression that they are intoxicated. And as is well documented by the boys, appearing not to care about how you look, partying, and being pictured with girls are three key markers of manliness. All of these messages send important signals about Noah's masculinity in spite of his emphasis on just presenting the authentic self.

Claiming that they are just showing the "real" self and emphasizing authenticity allows teen boys a cover for their self-narrative work, work they deem

Figure 3.6 Noah's Timeline Picture

feminine. This is not to suggest that their quest for authenticity is disingenuous; I think they care a lot about being authentic, as is evident by the policing they do of their peers. However, I think the way authenticity is bounded with norms of masculinity allows them to ensure they can achieve their goals simultaneously; exploring the self while staying safely within the boundaries of the social group and masculine gender norms. Indeed, it is only in talking with them about their images that it becomes clear just how aware and strategic boys are, despite the fact that on the surface their images may appear to be less traditionally flattering, organized, or even helpful in creating a self-narrative.

Image curation: the masculine body in action

Boys' emphasis on masculinity makes the social media experience challenging for them, as it requires them to engage in many activities they deem "not manly," such as image creation (taking and posting pictures) and image curation. In particular, the medium's emphasis on the visual is new for boys, as they are now "on display" (Bordo 1999) physically. The notion of being judged physically is not an explicitly common or welcome experience for males. Bordo (1999) argues that being scrutinized physically is "incompatible with being a real male" (177) because it is ultimately "feminine to be on 'display'" (179). Yet this type of work, looking good and being on display in images for evaluation by their peers, is required of adolescent males on social media. Thus, for boys, the way to balance the need for good images with the masculine self-presentation is to depict the body in action, covered or not, through athletic or muscular images. Figure 3.7 is an example of Peter showcasing the body in action. Peter is posing and showcasing his body, but it feels different from the girls' posed body images. First, he appears to be posing for the person on the beach, not the photographer. Secondly, the pose is designed to be funny, indicating that he does not focus on his looks. Additionally, his image shows the body in action after surfing. This image highlights the body without the feminine attributes associated with the "body on display" images that Bordo (1999) describes, and which are often depicted in girls' bikini pictures.

Image curation: pictures with hot girls

Posting pictures with "hot girls" is an important masculinity status marker that I observed frequently in the boys' pictures. Virtually every boy in the study mentioned the value of having pictures with girls, preferably "hot girls," on your social media as a key means to signal masculinity. Kenny said that when selecting an image to post on Facebook, "like guys you'll. . . pick those pictures of you with attractive girls." Another boy said that if you are in a picture with a "normal girl it's just like 'Hmm' . . . if you're like in a picture with an attractive girl that people think is attractive then it's big. Because people can see like, 'Oh he can get an attractive girl.' . . . It's completely status." Interestingly, it seems that

Figure 3.7 Peter's "Body in Action" Picture

posing with the girl seems to imply you can "get" the girl. The boys reported that these pictures are status markers for both their male and female audiences. Peter explained it this way:

> It kind of works two ways. I think it would boost your image to other guys, which I kind of think is actually like the primary reason people do it. . . I mean you like, like commanding that respect for like hanging out with girls, hanging out with good-looking girls like that.

I asked if guys "command" more respect if the girl is attractive, and Peter said, "For sure. Um, and then there's the other side um, which is commanding respect from other girls, which is kind of funny." Peter uses powerful language to describe these images, saying that they are "commanding respect" from both boys and girls alike. He acknowledges that it is strange that girls like his pictures with other girls, but he attributes it to the "jealousy factor."

And their male peers acknowledge this status, either with likes or comments. In one of Kenny's pictures, he is posing with his arm around a girl that he described as "hot" in the interview. They are both looking right at the camera and smiling, and their bodies appear to be touching. He received many comments on this picture from his male peers; many of them referenced this link between posing with the girl and "getting" the girl. He received comments such as "atta boy Ken" or "get some Ken" from his male peers. The appeal of these images is that they show a guy as popular with girls, which does double duty as it affirms their position within the social boundaries via social belonging and gender conformity. Thus, in performing gender, they are simultaneously delineating the social group.

Image curation: idiot pictures

Boys also relish the opportunity to make themselves and their male friends look like idiots on social media. Masculine norms dictate that they should not care about looking good in pictures, but another powerful component of these idiot pictures is that they can be used to signal social connections. Boys work hard to make their friends look like idiots, not in a mean-spirited way, but just as part of male bonding. As Kenny said in his interview, "You never let your friends live down the stupid stuff they say." Thus, even these unflattering pictures serve a purpose as a masculine bonding mechanism for boys on social media.

The awkward but funny picture of Myles (Figure 3.8) was the first thing he mentioned in our interview, interrupting my introductions to ask, "Did you see the one of me with . . . " and went on to describe in great detail the context of this picture. In preparation for his team's banquet, the boys put together a slideshow of embarrassing pictures of team members, and one teammate posted this to Facebook. From the way he spoke about this image, it was clear that he liked it a lot. Although he knows that he does not look great (i.e., this is not traditionally posed or flattering), other important factors of masculinity and social belonging can be inferred from this image. This, then, becomes an important and flattering image in

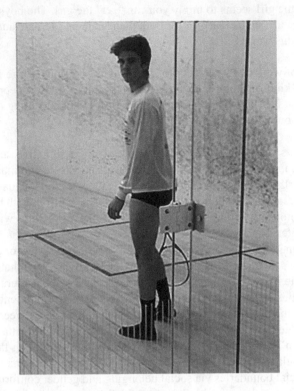

Figure 3.8 Myles' Picture From the Team Banquet

a different way; he appears masculine in his lack of concern about appearance and his athletic connections, and the image signals social belonging because a friend posted it for him.

Experiencing the images: social media actions

In addition to the images posted, masculinity norms apply to social media actions. Boys do not take pictures themselves, pose overtly in pictures, or take selfies, because they label these behaviors, and the overt emphasis on appearance that they signal, as feminine. This focus on the "manly" also plays out with likes. Boys do not like images or posts as frequently as girls do, explaining to me that they only do so when the images are very funny, amazing, or show attractive girls. They set this up as a feminine/masculine dichotomy, whereby it is feminine to like everything and therefore "normal" boys do not like things all the time.

By withholding likes, boys have incredible power over girls. Everyone acknowledged that likes are a form of approval, and therefore the fact that they do not like things all the time means that their likes are somehow more meaningful. Many of the girls mentioned that because female friends like everything they post, receiving the rare like from a boy actually means something. Kate described boys' likes in her interview:

> I think like for me it's like a much bigger deal if a boy likes it than a girl likes it. And I think boys are more inclined to like actual pretty shots, which like I wouldn't have thought, but then they actually do.

I asked her to clarify what she meant by "pretty shot" and she defined it as "close-up pretty pictures of you." She implies here that the pictures that the boys like are the "actual" pretty shots. What is important to consider here is what does that say about the other pictures, the ones that boys do not like? Are they, then, not pretty pictures? And of course, are these "actual pretty shots" that boys like simply transformed by this male approval? I do not have a clear answer to this, but it is worth mentioning, as many girls said some version of the "boys like the pretty pictures" statement. When I asked Kate about this in our interview, she explained it this way: she said that boys "definitely" like less in general, while in contrast "girls like everything." Because of this, she said that the boy's like "means more. . . Like yeah, it means like, 'Oh this is an actual pretty shot of me.'" Because "girls like everything," their likes are less helpful feedback. Kate actually did not learn anything new from her female friends' likes because their frequency seemed to negate their authenticity; rather, they were just being nice. In contrast, Kate said that a like from a boy meant that "this is an actual pretty shot of me." Boys avoid liking things to appear more masculine, and the result is that girls seek out their approval even more, thereby reinforcing traditional gender scripts and power dynamics inherent in the female quest for male approval. A like from a boy now means that the image is "actually" pretty.

Experiencing the images: mean in a funny way

As mentioned earlier in the book, outright cruelty on social media gets policed by boys on social media. It is important to note that everyone sees mean behavior, although almost all the teens were adverse to using the term "bullying" to describe the behavior, which perhaps indicates how loaded this word has become for this population. However, in spite of the fact that they all reported that mean words and images are shared on social media, I only observed boys confront mean behavior on social media. In fact, many girls reported that confronting people just is not something that is done on social media. In contrast, in my observation it appears that when these boys (or their friends) violate the rules of protocol and are cruel to each other, they are policed by each other and called out. One of the most overt examples of this that I observed was the experience that Kenny had in reaction to one of his pictures. For "Throwback Thursdays," where you post funny and/or embarrassing old pictures of yourself on social media, Kenny posted an image of him playing baseball as a young boy (Figure 3.9). Kenny received several comments asking if it was him or making friendly jokes, and then one boy posted a YouTube clip of a severely disabled young boy with the comment "hey guys it [*sic*] ken!"

Figure 3.9 Kenny's "Throwback Thursday" Baseball Picture

Over the course of the next several hours, four boys responded about the inappropriateness of this comment, saying "the line. . . it has been crossed," "you can't say that Mike," "mike thats not okay on so many levels," and "yeah smith that is not okay." Eventually, Kenny responded himself, saying, "you dont say that about a mentall[y] disabled kid." The original poster eventually responded saying, "Guys calm down I was saying the[y] look similar." While Mike's comments are inappropriate and mean-spirited at best, this moment is quickly and effectively policed by Kenny's friends and then eventually Kenny himself. When I asked Kenny about this experience, he said that this boy had given him trouble like this for a while, but noted that it did not bother him. He also noted the importance of his friends stepping in on social media: "So when they saw it they were like, 'Okay you're being an asshole so just stop.' So um, they kind of helped me with that because they, I think they saw that I was [dealing with this mean kid again]." Kenny felt that his friends were there to help him and stand up for him. Although the comment was awful, the fact that it was made public and visible allowed Kenny to find support in his peer group, which makes for a more positive outcome than may have been possible in a face-to-face interaction in this circumstance. Several boys said that it is hard to do this kind of thing face-to-face, but it feels a bit easier to call each other out on social media. Perhaps this is one example where hiding behind the screen is beneficial?

Boys routinely called out comments that were offensive and hurtful to the poster during the course of my observations. These are in contrast to the funny or sarcastically mean comments that boys regularly use and appreciate. In response to a football picture Chris posted of himself on the field in his uniform crouched in a football stance, one boy commented, "looks like your posing to take a dump on the 20 yard line" to which another boy responded "better than a piss on the bench!" Both of these comments were very well received by viewers and received their own likes from uninvolved Facebook friends. This interchange is funny and not damaging to Chris, and in the interview he told me he thought the whole thing was hilarious. Indeed, in many instances, sarcastic comments received more likes than the original picture.

However, it is worth noting that not all meanness is catalogued on social media. Many boys and girls mentioned that they talk offline with their peers about things that they see online. They told me that they will often have conversations with friends that include statements like, "Did you see what this person posted?" A few girls also reported screenshotting images/posts and then sending them to friends later to mock people. So, interestingly, the girls are willing to bring the mean offline, but they do not address mean things that happen to them in a visible way on social media.

Experiencing the images: homophobic comments to confirm masculinity

Jeff had a picture on his timeline that showed a profile of his face with his left hand up giving the audience the finger. Written on the picture (i.e., not a caption) was "Queen of deep throat" in white letters. Gay slurs like the one on Jeff's picture were deemed acceptable by the boys, because these comments were mostly targeted at close friends. Research indicates the use of homosexual slurs is a common occurrence among teen boys. In Pascoe's (2007) seminal work on adolescent masculinity, she writes that males engage with the "threatening specter of the faggot" to "affirm to themselves and each other that they are straight" (51), and importantly not feminine or weak. Thus, gay comments are not only acceptable, but are actually used among straight males as a way to affirm their heterosexuality. I saw fag and gay comments so frequently that I asked every boy about them in the follow-up interviews. While they each acknowledged that they know it is wrong to use these slurs, they explained it away by saying that it is "how we talk," "what guys say," or "we aren't calling the person gay, more the action." They were all quick to clarify that they would never use this language with "someone who is actually gay," but rather use it to describe close straight friends. When I asked Kenny in the interview what he thinks when he sees these comments, he said, "I see it, and I'm just like, 'Yeah they're really good friends that like messing with each other.'" He went on to say that he understands: "I, I, 'cause being a guy I can see why they're saying it like when you're best friends with another guy you just rip on him. And when, but you don't call anyone else faggot, you don't say that." For Kenny, not only does it affirm heterosexuality, it also confirms friendships.

Figure 3.10   "The Two Biggest Fags in the School"

Chris' picture (Figure 3.10) was one of a whole series of formal pictures that were posted by a girl and appeared as tagged pictures on his timeline. The image received the comment "two biggest fags in the school" from another boy.

Although this comment seems to echo Pleck's (1981) notion of men competing over manliness, Chris was fine with the comments, explaining: "That's just, that was our best friend joking around. . . probably just trying to give us a hard time." When I asked if it had anything to do with their formal attire or pose, Chris said he thought the friend was doing it "just in general trying to put each other down, just joking around." I believe Chris accepts the gay comment because it is a strategy boys use to delineate boundaries around masculinity, as they all said that they would not use the word to describe a gay person. Thus by using this word to describe a friendship between two heterosexual males dressed up and sitting close together on a couch, they can reconfirm their masculinity despite their emotional and physical closeness. It sends the message that in spite of engaging with the "threatening specter" (Pascoe 2007) of feminine behaviors, they are "manly." In this way, use of the word "fag" asserts their masculinity.

Gendered categories of worth

Walther (2008) argues that Facebook just reinforces traditional gender stereotypes. While this may be the end result, I think this happens because the categories of worth created in adolescence are gendered to favor femininity in girls and masculinity in boys. What typically is valued is a feminine girl and a masculine boy. As such, the self-narrative work must assert and enact these gender roles as well. The girls emphasize femininity in selected typologies (e.g., bikini shots), in their actions (e.g., comments and likes to friends), and in their experiences with their own images and feedback. The boys do the same, emphasizing masculinity in images (sports, pictures with girls) and actions (not liking images, appearing not to care, and sarcastic meanness). To have these visuals, they must be actively engaging in these actions. This is what may ultimately lead us to Walther's (2008) conclusion that social media reinforces gender stereotyping.

It is important to note that these findings on boys' use of homophobic slurs may be limited first and foremost by the fact that the data reflects only a small in-depth sample comprised of largely White, middle-class youths. I collected the data in 2012; indeed, boys' values may have evolved as the gay and transgender movements have gained more traction since the data was collected. Therefore, their stories, images, and internalization processes may not be representative of American males more generally, either then or in 2017. In particular, as Entwistle and Mears (2012) note, the notion that posing and looking good is feminine behavior is based on a predominately White male construction of masculinity. Although the male who identified as Black was one of the most vocal about the need to appear masculine, it is likely that these findings describe a largely White male phenomenon.

Also, my data is focused primarily on a male/female binary gender construction and cannot at this time speak to transgender, questioning, or transitioning adolescents. Butler argues that gender should not be "reducible to hierarchical heterosexuality" (2004: 54), and to address this critique, I attempted to consider the ways in which non-heteronormative behaviors play out on social media. This was a challenge, given both the medium and age group. Status in adolescence is conferred through heteronormative gender performances, which may encourage heteronormative conformity by all teens regardless of sexual orientation (Pascoe 2007). Although I cannot be certain of the reasons, I did not observe anyone who did not conform to heteronormative gender rules, regardless of sexuality.

Ultimately, I believe certain story typologies are more powerful in the creation of the fable than others; political awareness or travel were mentioned by participants as showing that a person was engaged and doing "cool" things, but these did not seem to affect the fable or confirm one's position in the social group. In contrast, the gender story seems to have significant influence on one's fable, and the power of the gendered norms shows that gender plays an important role in affirming one's position in the group. Performing masculinity or femininity is important is defining the self and affirming acceptance in a social group. The key gendered stories emphasize traditional gender scripts, which means that in many ways, social media is simply providing teens a new way to enact traditional gender roles and scripts. Thus, the traditional processes of gendered self-definition have not changed significantly since West and Zimmerman (1987), Gilligan (1982, 1987), and Butler (1990) wrote about them 30 or 40 years ago.

Notes

1 This is the girls' abbreviation for profile pictures.
2 The girls defined "high likes" people as individuals on social media who are known for getting a lot of likes. The logic here is that if you post a picture with someone who gets a lot of likes (and tag him or her in the picture), you will benefit from his or her likes and get a lot yourself. All the girls had sense of individuals who are "high likes" people; they just get a lot of likes on everything they post.
3 This is the girls' abbreviation for photographer credits.

References

Armstrong, Elizabeth A., Laura Hamilton, and Brian Sweeney. 2006. "Sexual Assault on Campus: A Multilevel, Integrative Approach to Party Rape" *Social Problems* 53: 483–499.

Bogle, Kathleen A. 2008. *Hooking Up, Sex, Dating, and Relationships on Campus*. New York, NY: New York University Press.

Bordo, Susan. 1999. *The Male Body: A New Look at Men in Public and in Private*. New York, NY: Farrar, Straus and Giroux.

Butler, Judith. 1990. *Gender Trouble*. New York, NY: Routledge.

———. 2004. *Undoing Gender*. New York, NY: Routledge.

Connell, R. W. 1995. *Masculinities*. Cambridge, UK: Polity Press.

Connell, R. W. and James Messerschmidt. 2005. "Hegemonic Masculinities" *Gender and Society* 19 (6): 829–859.

Crick, Nicki R. and Jennifer K. Grotpeter. 1995. "Relational Aggression, Gender, and Social-Psychological Adjustment" *Child Development* 66 (3): 710–722.

Davis, Jenny and Nathan Jurgenson. 2011. "Prosuming Identity Online" in *Cyborgology*, edited by Nathan Jurgenson and P. J. Rey. http://thesocietypages.org/cyborgology/

Dunbar, Robin. 1998. *Grooming, Gossip, and the Evolution of Language*. Cambridge, MA: Harvard University Press.

Entwistle, Joanne and Ashley Mears. 2012. "Gender on Display: Performativity in Fashion Modeling" *Cultural Sociology* 7 (3): 320–335.

Gilligan, Carol. 1982. *In a Different Voice: Psychological Theory and Women's Development*. Cambridge, MA: Harvard University Press.

———. May 1987. "Adolescent Development Reconsidered" 10th Annual Konopka Lecture.

Goffman, Erving. 1959. *The Presentation of Self in Everyday Life*. New York, NY: Anchor Books, Doubleday.

Hamilton, Laura. 2007. "Trading on Heterosexuality: College Women's Gender Strategies and Homophobia" *Gender and Society* 21: 145–172.

Jurgenson, Nathan and P. J. Rey. 2013. "The Fan Dance: How Privacy Thrives in an Age of Cyber-Publicity" in *Unlike Us Reader: Social Media Monopolies and Their Alternatives,* edited by Geert Lovink and Miriam Rasch. Amsterdam: Institute of Network Cultures.

Kimmel, Michael. 1994. "Masculinity as Homophobia: Fear, Shame and Silence in the Construction of Gender Identity" in *Feminism and Masculinities,* edited by Peter F. Murphy. Cambridge, UK: Cambridge University Press.

Mears, Ashley. 2011. *Pricing Beauty: The Making of a Fashion Model*. Berkeley, CA: University of California Press.

Miller, Jean B. 1976. *Toward a New Psychology of Women*. Boston, MA: Beacon Press.

Pascoe, C. J. 2007. *Dude You're a Fag: Masculinity and Sexuality in High School*. Berkeley, CA: University of California Press.

Pleck, Joseph H. 1981. *The Myth of Masculinity*. Cambridge, MA: MIT Press.

Surrey, Janet. 1980. *Self-in-Relation: A Theory of Women's Development*. Wellesley, MA: Stone Center for Developmental Services and Studies.

Thorne, Barrie. 1993. *Gender Play: Girls and Boys in School*. New Brunswick, NJ: Rutgers University Press.

Walther, Joseph B. 2008. "The Role of Friends' Appearance and Behavior on Evaluations of Individuals on Facebook: Are We Known by the Company We Keep? *Human Communication Research* 34 (1): 28–49.

West, Candace and Don H. Zimmerman. 1987. "Doing Gender" *Gender and Society* 1: 125–151.

Wiseman, Rosalind. 2002. *Queen Bees and Wannabees*. New York, NY: Random House Inc.

4 The synthesis of the real and the reel me

Many have written about how we "type the self into being" on social media (Sunden 2003: 3, see also boyd and Ellison 2007, Marwick and boyd 2014). I would amend this to add that we also visualize ourselves into being via our images. As one of the teens said, "'cause pictures speak a lot of words. . . I wanted to share that [image]." This adds a different layer to Sunden's analysis because images require a great deal of backstage work to create and curate the visual self. Through this process, teens engage in both an outer and inner reveal, to revisit the fan dance analogy (Jurgenson and Rey 2012). The outer reveal work involves syncing the highlights reel created to give off a positive impression to the audience to the notion of the "real me now" that exists in their minds in the personal fable, all while ensuring that the gender and social norms are followed. While that in and of itself sounds like a great deal of work, the inner reveal is more complicated in some regards. The work of the inner reveal of the self cannot be minimized and is perhaps the greatest affordance of Facebook or Instagram technology for teens. This is perhaps a positive component to social media. While the narrative in American society tends to focus a lot on the negative aspects of teens' social media use, it is important to acknowledge the potential for a benefit to social media use. And indeed, this is not unique to Facebook or Instagram; this benefit could be true of other types of emerging and social media that ask users to create a visual presentation of the self. This inner work is hard to measure in typical ways via surveys or interviews, and therefore it is often overlooked. By observing teens' postings and then speaking to them about specific images, I was able to see this inner work that often gets obscured by the front stage highlights reel of their social media images. During the portion of the interviews where I asked the teens to talk about their images, I asked them to simply "Tell me the story of this picture" or "How did this picture come to be on Facebook?" Becker (2003) argues that an important component of visual sociology is to analyze how the image came to be. I adapted this to address both the story of how the image came to be and how it ended up on Facebook. I believe that these interview questions allowed the participants to construct their narratives around the meaning of the image and the process of curating it for social media. It was in these moments that I could hear them describe the inner work that they engaged in through these processes.

The outer reveal, the focus of the previous chapters, involves the presentation of the self to the generalized other (Mead 1962). While this looks like the highlights reel, this presentation is important as it confirms to the teens that they are social beings and socially accepted by the group. They use the guideposts they learn via social media to ensure that they present the self as part of a social group. This can be done in many ways—literally through images with friends that show social belonging, and more subtly by following cues to ensure that their image typologies match up with those of their social group (e.g., the duck face images). They also adhere to fairly strict norms of hypermasculinity and hyperfemininity that signal their gender conformity to the audience. While boys and girls may have a variety of interests and proclivities, they tend to curate their images to ensure that gender conformity is clear and unquestioning. A large part of the outer reveal to the generalized other is the confirmation of social and gender conformity.

The rigidity of social and gender conformity makes it hard to believe there is any unique inner, or perhaps arguably even any important, work being done here. After all, if they are just conforming to the group, how could their social media presence represent the "real me"? This is a logical critique, and was my initial thought upon seeing these images, too. Everything seemed so redundant, it was hard to see anything more than the worst aspects of the high school experience. And while I do not deny or try to ignore the existence of those negative moments, I think it does not represent the full spectrum of their experiences. And ultimately I think even these difficult parts of adolescence are parts of the experience, if perhaps less appealing to see visually on social media. First, signaling belonging, even if we do it with pictures in matching clothes, is really important, perhaps to all of us, but certainly to adolescents. As Erikson (1980) described, at this point in their lives adolescents are beginning to construct the self in the context of their relationships with their peers. While the self is, of course, socially constructed in all contexts, Erikson highlights the notion that the social self comes to preeminence in adolescence. As such, figuring out the self in relation to the peer group is a critical component of adolescent self-development work; conforming images in their highlights reel, and the blatant quest for likes, both have value for the development of the self. So what we see as conformity in image is really key work to signal social belonging. As observers we can wish it looked different, but it is something that has mattered in adolescence for generations, and I think it would be naive to assume that it would change in the social media era.

Their presentation is also bounded by gender scripts, as the importance of showing performances that highlight masculinity in boys and femininity in girls is profound. So much of what the teens posted during my observation period was filtered through a gender-scripted performance; while everyone needs to look good on social media, what it means to look good is highly gendered. And additionally, what you can do to get the pictures is also gendered. Thus, gender norms are central in every phase of the process, from image creation to image posting.

Yet in spite of the significance of gender norms for every phase of the process, I observed variability with which these teens adhered to these social and gender rules on social media. While all the teens I observed seemed to intuitively know these rules and follow them to some degree, there was real variability in terms of their consistency and the extent to which they adhered to the rules. Some were strict followers, with images that rarely diverged from the norm. Others had these pictures, but interspersed with them were images that pushed the boundaries of the rules and appear to be more about the individual asserting the self independent from the group. An example of this was a very atypical photo shoot Diana, a very smart 18-year-old with a biting sense of humor, engaged in that simultaneously mocked photo shoots and asserted her as different via challenging the gender norms. In the images, she's on a playground, where she is posing on the different playground equipment. She is posed and not smiling, but she does not conform to the typical model posing or style. Hers is more of a goth take, or spoof really, on the arty/model poses. She said that she "absolutely" took and posted these pictures to make fun of the girls who do photo shoots "for real" to get images for social media. She talked about doing the poses they do, but intentionally looking "really weird" (by staring at the camera, without a smile, on playground equipment). This is her chance to challenge some of the norms around appearance and femininity. Thus while these teens follow the rules for the most part, there are places where we can see them challenge the norms. And the reasons for this can be as simple as a desire to challenge them because they think they are ridiculous, as in the case of Noah and Diana, or because they are of high social status, as in the case of Gebre's "borderline selfie," which he knows he can "get away with" on social media. Regardless, there is more than just uniform acceptance of the social and gender rules.

Ultimately, I think there is room for both a fairly proscriptive narrative that focuses on confirming social and gender belonging and an opportunity to test norms to present the self and assert unique aspects of the personal fable. And there are opportunities to do as much or as little of each as they deem worthwhile at the time; in fact, they can easily oscillate between the two depending on their experiences, stage of development, and feelings at the time. When I asked one of the 18-year-old boys for the story of why he selected his profile picture, he first listed off the aspects of the pictures that worked to ensure his social and gender belonging: he thought he looked good in the picture, the picture was taken at a "cool event" but it was not a selfie, and generally it was a good picture (lighting, centered on him, etc.). But then he said that one of the things that is important to him in selecting a profile picture is that "the picture I have has to show like who I am because [otherwise] then. . . they won't know who I am." He is doing both types of work here—he is conforming to many standards of masculinity here and yet also presenting the version of the self that he thinks really shows people "who I am." The ways teens use these two categories of images are not the same for everyone, but that is the beauty of it. Wherever they are in the self-development process, the affordances of social media technology enable them to visualize the self and project it to others.

Because of this, I invite you to reserve judgment; the time they spend taking pictures and posting them to social media is valuable. While some of this work is indeed purely to highlight the physical self and get attention, and to be sure the social media experiences are not uniformly positive, the power of using the public space to curate "the self into being" (Sunden 2003: 3) cannot be minimized. And indeed, it is something, at least in the curation phase, that they can create. One girl in the mixed-age focus group described social media as something that is "in your control"—unlike so much that happens face-to-face. Another girl talked about how social media gives you the opportunity to "choose how to present yourself." Both of these girls are talking about social media giving them a sense of control over their self-presentation, which can be hard to manage in face-to-face synchronous interactions.

John (2013) calls sharing on Web 2.0 an "act of communication" (115). On these social media platforms, what gets shared most frequently are images. And these teens all described their images as a communication tool; the effort they put into the performance, their awareness of how the performance will land before the audience even sees it, and the desire to present the authentic self on social media, which they all share, leads me to believe that social media is important. It is a tool for communicating the self to their peers, and ultimately to themselves as well.

This is on display in a very obvious way in Gebre's picture (Figure 4.1), in which he showcases his multi-ethnicity; his Ethiopian and Muslim cultures represented in his clothes, and his American culture peeking out in his socks. When I asked him about this image and why he selected it for social media, he told me that the image was created specifically to post online and then talked about wanting to use the platform to show different aspects of his self-story. He does not wear this combination of dress to school, as he attends a school that has a dress code. As such, the kids at school do not see him in Ethiopian dress, and indeed he makes it clear that none would ever see it except for the fact that the architecture of the social media platform enables him to highlight this side of himself there. It breaks some gender rules in that it is clearly a posed picture that he had taken specifically for Facebook. He wants us to see this on social media. And importantly for our understanding, his religious and ethnic identities are deeply important to his story of the self and therefore he wants an image to show this.

We spent a lot of time in the interview talking about the ways that his ethnicity, religion, and class affect his social media experiences. He talked about seeing pictures of his school peers on these amazing vacations that he and his family cannot afford. He talked about the fact that most of his school friends just see him in a coat and tie at school and have no sense of his Muslim and Ethiopian heritages. Similarly, his family and friends from his Ethiopian community have no sense of his life in private school. He cares about all of these audiences, and strategizes his pictures given that he has "an audience that is very wide" on social media. Because so many pictures get taken in school contexts (sports, friend pictures, etc.), he wants to make sure that he is seen as more than just a prep school kid. He laughed, saying that many of his current pictures are "like of me in a shirt and tie with my friends from school." This picture stands in stark contrast. In the

Figure 4.1   Gebre's Timeline Photo

following excerpt from his interview, he highlights the importance of his unique personal fable:

> And some will not understand them, but I think by now, I think I work on making sure people like understand like that I have. . . that it's not just like, I'm not like one-dimensional. . . I think people understand like this will like go to what I do and. . . I make sure that people know that about me so that they understand because I don't want them just thinking you know, something.

Gebre's response shows the inner and outer reveal of his image; he thinks both about how it will be received by others and about what it means for him. It matters to Gebre that he is not seen as a "stereotype of a Pierce School" kid because in his personal fable he is "more than that." He is aware that not everyone will understand the image; in fact, he says some of his school friends might respond with "What the hell is going on?" although his Muslim friends will totally understand it. But Gebre is not worried if there is confusion among some, as the goal with this image is not simply to assure social and gender belonging. This image does not look like many of his peers' images, and in spite of the lack of understanding of the image by his peer audience, he wants to present this largely private multidimensionality and is entirely aware of how different this image will feel on social media. In an interesting way, social media enables Gebre to showcase a piece of himself that is not easily visible in his face-to-face interactions with peers at school who never see him dressed like this. Social media allows him to control his presentation of the self and provides him the space to think through the way the image speaks to his self-conception.

Gebre also has a picture of himself on a service learning project working with kids. This trip was very important to him, and we spent a lot of time talking about it, as it is directly connected to many of the things he is involved with during the school year. On the surface, beyond being a "cool trip," this image does not fit many of the typical norms—Gebre is not showcasing social belonging or his masculinity, things that he is hypervigilant about in his more typical pictures. But when I asked him about this picture with the kids, he said, "So like that represents me and like you know who I am and who I want to be so I like. . . that." He then went on to tell me all about the kids that he visited at this orphanage and said that he received this picture at the end of his trip and decided to post it himself. In the image caption he refers to the boys in the picture as "my brothers." So these moments of self-reflection and thought about the self really do matter in some cases. This is an image that, for Gebre, "represents me," and I would argue that when kids find those images (and they can work within the boundaries of the rules), they have a powerful moment of self-confirmation.

Another boy told me about how he really "evolved" as a person from when he first started high school. He attributed this evolution to his interest in a sport, which he referred to during the interview as "my identity." He talked about how most of his pictures now showcase him doing that sport—either by himself or with his team—because it means so much to him. While of course this is not his entire identity, it is the part of his identity that at this moment is most salient for him; hence that is what he is showing now in visual images. These pictures serve him well in terms of highlighting the body in action and conforming to other masculinity norms around athletics, but for him, it feels like a totally authentic representation of "my identity." And again, the work for us is not to determine whether it is authentic, but rather to understand that it feels that way for him, hence giving it power and meaning in his life.

I have argued against an online versus offline dichotomy; however, the work in the social media creation phase, where teens take and curate their pictures, is the one place where I see a difference in their online versus offline interactions. Because there is no set timeline for posting pictures in this creation phase, teens can create a strategic and controlled social media presentation and internalize these experiences. The way they use the technology in the creation phase allows them to think through the presentation of the self and be far more strategic than they can in offline interactions, which require immediate responses and are harder to control.

What gets presented: the evolving self in the social media context

I think it is best to think of social media as a tool that teens can adapt as they need on their developmental path; depending on how and how fully they have conceptualized the self, they may use these sites in different ways and also make and take different meanings from them. The perception of the self can and will change according to teens' experiences and over time. As a result, the personal fable that adolescents present on social media really documents the evolving self; it is the image (or images) of the self as they conceptualize it in that moment: the real me now. Because the self evolves gradually and with many stops and starts on the developmental pathway, it requires a lot of their attention and time. I think this is one of the reasons that social media is such a time-intensive draw for adolescents. While they are looking for feedback from peers once the image is posted, they are also spending a lot of time preparing the visual representation of the self as they see it in that moment. Some described the fun and power they feel in doing this work either in consultation with their friends or "alone in their pajamas." Others found it more confusing and fraught. In part because it is so confusing and also, too, because all these starts and stops are now documented visually on social media. And of course, because no one likes to be called out for their mistakes, there is a real desire to ensure that they get it right, however they conceptualize that at the time. It is not a stress-free experience by any means.

In addition to these stressors, however, the technology does allow for the one pause in the prosumption (Davis and Jurgenson 2011) process in which they can think through how they want to present the self now, which of course may be different from prior or later presentations. As mentioned previously, they report feeling "in control" of the curation and creation of social media images. To be sure, there are aspects of the social media feedback that they cannot control, such as comments, screenshots, and judgments, but they can control what they choose to present. This is powerful for adolescents and cannot be minimized, as so much of their experiences are outside of their control.

What is interesting to me is that although they shed the earlier version of the self as they grow, they leave these versions of the self, albeit perhaps deleting the most awkward images, on the public forum of Facebook. They look at these old images from time to time much like adults might look at an old photo album to reminisce. They laugh and cringe about their earlier selves and told me that it is a "red flag" if you do not have any old pictures on your social media, as it seems like you "did not exist" earlier. As much as they want to show the current highlights reel, they also want to show the old highlights reels. They place value on documenting earlier iterations of the self and looking back at them because the evolution of the self plays an important role in their fables; capturing the evolving self on Facebook allows for a "look how I have changed" self-dialogue and perhaps even explains the obsession they share with posting pictures of themselves as babies or small children, which universally receive a lot of likes on these platforms. Lucy said these baby pictures are appealing "'cause it's cute you know and. . . like a little different age when you can actually see them in it. . . especially people that are annoying now and act like such a teenager it's like 'aw that was them once.'" They like to see others' evolving selves, and they really like to see their own evolution. While they may delete their most embarrassing pictures from when they were younger, they, especially the girls, reported that it is really fun to look back at social media and see how much they have changed and grown. They like this opportunity to reflect on the self, and it was interesting to me that many of them spoke about doing this sporadically (in moments of boredom, etc.), but especially in moments of key life transitions—the start and end of high school, the end of summer, and so forth. At these times, when they get to start anew, they seemed to like to go back to look at their old images. While many joked about how "dorky" or "stupid" they used to be, they always said this with humor and appreciation for where they are now. Ultimately, these depictions of the evolving self are one of the reasons they see the social media presentation as more than just the highlights reel; their images show changes, growth, and even some slip-ups, but teens leave them there because documenting the evolving self in this way showcases their development, which may serve to build confidence; they get to see that the self is evolving, for the most part in a positive way, which is something that may positively impact their sense of self.

This theory of the evolving self and the time and effort that adolescents spend in documenting it on social media also suggests a gap in the current sociobiological research on the adolescent brain. Research has shown that the slow development of the frontal cortex in adolescence leads to less impulse control and self-reflection (Cooney 2010; Ruder 2008; National Institute of Mental Health 2011). These findings, while well supported via scientific testing, have been applied to social media to assume that because of poor impulse control and technology that allows for immediate picture taking, uploading of images, and comments, teenagers will post images and comments with no forethought or awareness of the consequences. While my research does not speak to or detract from any of the brain research findings, it does suggest that the findings may not be generalizable to the entirety of teens' social media experiences as a whole.[1]

While images and comments that lack forethought and judgment were evident on these teens' Facebook, especially when they reported drinking during the time of picture taking and posting, this type of experience did not outnumber their highly strategic and thoughtful presentations.[2] Because the brain research has become such a powerful and important narrative in the field of adolescent development, I believe researchers risk making assumptions about adolescent behaviors that discount the awareness they have of their evolving self and their online presentation of the self. This research shows that, while they may not always do so, they are capable of making thoughtful choices, which is perhaps made easier because of the technological affordances of social media that allow them some time and space to think before posting a new picture. This is particularly evident in the fact that they spend so much of their time in the creation phase. Beyond the scope of this research, I wonder: Does technology have the potential to alter the brain, or at the very least heighten this awareness of self in adolescents? And if so, how do we teach adolescents to reap the positive benefits of this awareness?

Social media provides teens an opportunity for inner and outer feedback on the evolving self. The inner work involves answering whether they like what they see in the visual presentation (i.e., does this visually depicted story of the self align with the story in one's mind). I describe this as internal feedback. The outer work involves following the social rules, receiving likes, and having many friends or followers on social media. I call this external feedback on the self. Both are important to these adolescents' conceptions of the self, and they can work together to affirm or negate the evolving self.

Feedback and the evolving self

As I mentioned at the start of this chapter, at the micro level adolescent development is influenced by social interactions, which take place offline, on social media, or, as my participants reported, sometimes online and offline simultaneously. Adolescents receive feedback on all of these social interactions. What happens offline can affect what you can present as your social media narrative (i.e., what you are able to present), the interactions that your posts generate (i.e., likes and comments), and how you process this experience (i.e., internalization of the feedback). The same can be said for the influence of social media interactions on offline interactions. Thus, the offline and online are deeply intertwined in teens' consciousness and end up in a mutually reinforcing relationship in terms of what teens present, the feedback they get, and how they internalize that feedback. This makes sense and is further support of the notion that there is no easy separation between offline and online.

What is on display on social media is the public looking-glass self. In Cooley's (1964) concept of the looking-glass self, he argued that individuals develop this through an understanding of others' perceptions of them. For Cooley, the individual uses social interactions to understand how others see him; this understanding in turn influences how he sees himself. But in Cooley's theory, the interpretive work he described was largely individual work. Social media technology has made this work visible to others, thus creating a public looking glass. While social interactions and others' perceptions (on or offline) still help to form the self, these mirrors we use to evaluate the self are now made public. Thus, the looking-glass self is a public discourse on social media. Making these mirrors public may be the draw and danger of social media for adolescents; they have to get the presentation right because it is out there for everyone to see and judge, and there is such potential for it all to go wrong. Yet as boyd (2014) notes, for the most part the "kids are all right" and they manage this well. While I certainly saw examples in the study of times when the fable presentation did go wrong, interestingly it was only in one or two cases. For the majority of the kids in the study, and indirectly their peers who engaged with and on my participants' images during the observation period, they were by and large getting it right. This actually is an incredible achievement in adolescence; they are on social media so much and managing to get it right so often that saying that the kids are "all right" is really no small feat.

The social media friend feedback loop

The feedback loop from friends on social media is fairly straightforward, and is received via likes, comments, and other forms of interaction on one's feed. Because the feedback on social media is not face-to-face, it can feel removed and perhaps less authentic than offline interactions, and therefore is often discounted in the literature (see Turkle 2007; Holson 2014; Kraut et al. 1998). Indeed, this "one to many" communication style can seem "unsubstantial" in many ways because interactions are often brief and broadcast for all social media friends or followers to see (Boneva et al. 2006). While it is beyond the scope of my data to posit the relative influence of these Facebook interactions on the evolving self, my work makes it clear that this feedback is important to adolescents and should not be dismissed as "unsubstantial." All participants stated that likes are important to them and that feedback, even negative feedback, is better than nothing, because it means that you matter. While we can wish that feedback from peers did not matter as much as it does, as Erikson (1980) notes, attention to social belonging in adolescence is nothing new. While the quest for social belonging may be more visibly obvious to us given the likes feature on social media—and indeed a concern about obtaining a certain number of likes is unique to the social media experience—it is not creating a new concern in adolescence, just amplifying it visually. Adolescents visually document their social capital for their Facebook friends and, perhaps as importantly, for themselves to see.

While they have a preconceived notion of their social capital in their internal narrative irrespective of social media, this technological architecture gives teens a chance to test out this narrative of their social worth and in most cases confirm their position. Once the image goes live on social media, they can see the interactions that their posts generate, interpret the meanings of the likes and comments they receive, and, to use their term, see "how well it does" on social media. In the follow-up interviews, I asked how these teens felt about seeing likes and other interactions on some of their pictures, and while a few referenced the importance of other people seeing the number of likes they received, the majority stated that the stress is not about everyone else seeing how many likes you get, but seeing the number for yourself. Kate reported that she likes to get around 40 likes for her profile pictures. When I asked her why she wanted so many likes, she said that that number would "mean that I was in the group." In other words, the likes are a visual confirmation of group membership for Kate. This is not a number she settled on with friends, but rather one she decided on for herself.

For boys, who receive fewer likes in general, the findings are not as straightforward because they cannot use likes as the main confirmation of social position. However, the goofy and ridiculous pictures that boys post of their friends, such as the one Myles' friend posted of him on the squash court with his shorts and socks hiked up as high as possible, serve the same purpose. Kenny described these goofy pictures as "we look like idiots. . . like it's not like we're trying" to adhere to masculine norms about appearance and "trying too hard." While this is just the "real me," in reality these boys are actually trying very hard to showcase the "real me" in the context of group membership and masculine conformity. The goofiness of the tone belies the importance of this work. When boys post pictures of their friends, even when they look silly, it is as if they are giving the person a like, just done in a way that conforms to masculinity norms on social media. While the girls rushed to check likes, Myles rushed to tell me about his silly picture, literally interrupting my interview introduction to talk about it, because it was meaningful for him in a similar way. After listening to Myles talk about it for a while it became clear that for him, this image showed his peer and self audience that he is part of a team, has friends, and is in on the joke that he looks ridiculous. In a way, this image gives Myles a thumbs-up in the same way that a like may do for some of the other kids in the study; it gives him confirmation that these important aspects of his presentation are visible and understood by the audiences.

I ended my interview with Kenny by asking him about the mean-spirited comment he received on his Throwback Thursday baseball picture, in which the commenter essentially likened Kenny to someone with significant intellectual and physical disabilities. In particular, we talked about the fact that Kenny's friends stood up for him in their comments. Kenny reports that their actions "kind of helped me." Although Kenny never got more than a dozen likes on any of his images, this visible support from friends meant a great deal to him. While this had the potential to be a self-negating experience for Kenny, and certainly their support does not negate the bullying, it did turn this into an affirming moment in terms of social belonging, one from which he could derive confidence and feelings of self-worth from the peer support he could see via the Facebook technology. When the public discourse around the visual presentation of the self results in positive feedback, which can happen in the form of likes, more images with friends, and other ways, it can affirm social competency. In this group of adolescents, social competency depends on social belonging and gender conformity. The teens talked about the experiences of seeing this affirmation of the self, and of looking back at old posts to see those as affirmation as well. Although beyond the scope of this research, I think it is possible that this process can result in positive effects on self-confidence.

Of course, this is not a uniform experience. While my participants were rarely the victim of bullying, there were subtle moments when the feedback (or lack thereof) did not affirm the self. In his interview Max talked a lot about his involvement with competitive cycling; almost every point he made either referenced his cycling or used cycling as a generic example (i.e., "say you took a picture of me riding"). In particular, he noted that in the last two years, during which time his commitment to competitive cycling has grown exponentially, social media has presented an interesting way to evaluate his friendships. He said that most of his peers from school do not know about his cycling and/or do not really understand the sport. As such, when he posts things like "Great weather for a century today" on social media, most of his friends do not get it. When he sees this it makes him question his friendships. He says that in "the process of having to explain myself I kind of ostracize myself from them because they feel like if they don't know what I'm talking about then they're not as good of friends with me as they should be." For Max, this process enables both sides to see distance in their friendship. With his new interest Max's posts are moving away from a group of friends, and as he noted, seeing it on social media allows him both to think about who he is (Is he a cyclist? Is that who he wants to be?) and to evaluate that in the context of his social belonging. This kind of inner dialogue, prompted by the visual presentation and assessment, is an interesting component of the social media process.

Social media as a mechanism for inner dialogue

I have talked about the peer feedback that occurs once a picture goes live on social media and how this can be internalized in a way that either affirms or challenges the evolving self; however, there is another important type of feedback, an internal dialogue that the Facebook presentation cultivates in the initial creation phase. This feedback has been overlooked in the literature largely because of the methods employed in social media research to date. Because a large portion of the follow-up interviews were devoted to the story and meanings of their images, I was able understand the hard work they do in anticipation of posting on social media. What my findings highlight is that the inner dialogue begins before the image is even posted to the site and is independent, at least in the beginning, from the feedback they receive from others. The self-dialogue they engage in when they are creating the presentation is different from the reflective work adolescents engage in once the image has been posted to social media and they receive peer feedback and make determinations about their presentation.

Facebook and Instagram facilitate this inner dialogic process because they are primarily visual platforms; in addition to showing the personal fable to others, you can actually see your own visual representation of your inner narrative as you create it. While the personal fable exists in your mind irrespective of social media, this technology adds a new component to the fable, one that has important consequences for adolescent development; in essence, social media is a public space that fosters inner dialogue. Teens strive to match the public presentation with their inner dialogue, and this is in large part what they are doing in the creation phase work; they see a visual of the story and evaluate how well it matches with their personal fable. The technological affordances allow them to visualize how successfully they have done this.

The first step in this creation phase self-dialogue is determining whether a Facebook performance matches with a self-story. This is the authenticity check, or to use my participants' language, this is where they determine whether they can "back it up online." So in other words, a teen might think she is part of a social group, but when she goes to present this on social media she will be forced to "back it up" with actual images that document this social connection. For the most part, this works out well, and teens post the images that match their story. Chris, the participant whose narrative was dominated by his athletic capabilities in high-status sports such as ice hockey and lacrosse, was able to post a picture capturing him in his lacrosse uniform with the caption "2 sports in the spring?" This was an easy decision for him, as the image matched the story he had in his head about who he is, and therefore affirmed this version of the self. He knew this before he even posted it. For Chris, this image becomes the "real me," and when this is coupled with the positive feedback he received from others in the form of six likes, high for a boy's non-profile picture in the study, and comments such as "kids a savage" from one of his male Facebook friends, the power this process has to foster confidence in the self is significant.

This works beautifully for cases like Chris', where an existing image fills an important role in confirming the positive aspect of the internal narrative. The question is, what happens when images do not match up with the highlights reel in the mind? In these cases, the image needed to convey the evolving story does not exist in advance of posting, and therefore it must be created expressly for social media. Although the image is "manufactured" then in a sense, it is still an important part of the self-dialogue process (i.e., what do you make of the mismatch between the images and the self-story, and also what can/should you do to reconcile the discrepancy?). Yet there is also a danger that these images may be viewed as less organic and authentic, although most teens accepted this provided that these images do not dominate the "given off" (Goffman 1959) impression of their front stage work.

While everyone creates images to some degree, there is a significant gender difference in how this plays out. In her interview, Cassie revealed that her self-narrative invoked a dual feminine/tomboy image. Without manufacturing images for Facebook, her visual self was more focused on her athletic and tomboy side, as these were the images readily available to her because of the plethora of team pictures and because she was often tagged in others' sports images. As a result, Cassie went out of her way to create and post a few images she deemed more feminine. She did this via posed bathroom mirror selfies, which all girls reported was more socially acceptable for younger girls than older girls. As Cassie was in eighth grade at the time she participated in this study, these images were considered acceptable for her. In many of her mirror selfies, she is posed in a stylized way to cultivate a feminine and sexualized image. She manufactured images like this in order to ensure the internal story she possessed of a tomboy/feminine self was presented on Facebook.

Again, there is some risk in manufacturing images, and Cassie seemed ambivalent about these pictures she created for Facebook, captioning one of these images "HAhahaha. Im so weird," indicating that she is not totally comfortable with the way she has reconciled her internal narrative and Facebook presentation. Even though this picture was in stark contrast to the goofy or more athletic images that dominated Cassie's Facebook, the gender rules that allow for photo shoots and glamorized selfies for girls mean that this was an acceptable image for her to have on Facebook, again as long as they do not dominate her feed. It is interesting to note that the image only received two likes (one from the other girl in the picture), which is considered low for girls, perhaps suggesting that her peers were ambivalent about this presentation as well.

Cassie used another tactic to reconcile these two versions of herself. In the following image (Figure 4.2), for instance, she blends the tomboy and feminine together in an interesting way. In this image, she is wearing her basketball uniform while posing provocatively holding a lollipop. The image illustrates the evolving self in this moment, as Cassie was clearly working through her story and deciding how to balance her feminine/tomboy persona. The image feels awkward to me as an adult because of the odd adult/child juxtaposition, but for Cassie, this is probably an accurate depiction of her evolving self as she envisioned it at this moment. Cassie captioned this image, "Posin in the bathroom. . . Casual." The use of the word "casual" intrigues me, as it could be her way of validating its authenticity (i.e., she does not work too hard for it) or it could be her way of reconciling her tomboy and feminine selves.

While boys who do not have the images to back up their self-story will also manufacture images, the gender rules do not allow them to do so as blatantly. They cannot take selfies or do photo shoots, and as a result they have to go to great lengths, such as photobombing pictures or relying on girls to post images. As a result, the boys' inner dialogic process is different. While girls like Cassie

Figure 4.2 Cassie's "Bathroom Mirror Selfie"

can display the work they do to create the image, boys have to make the picture happen in a way that appears effortless. But this is dangerous for boys because of the importance they place on authenticity. They police each other to ensure authenticity, and therefore they have to work very hard to ensure that an image does not veer too far from their real self. There are obvious social consequences—as they will be called out as "posers" by their peers, an example of which will be discussed in a subsequent section—but also consequences for the inner dialogue. How can they internalize an inauthentic self? This is one reason being authentic, even if it is an authenticity bounded by the rules of social media, is so important to them. They need to present something that they can truly recognize as the self. There is a genuine desire in them to really see themselves and explore who they are at a given moment, which can be harder for them to do in face-to-face interactions. While so much can influence face-to-face interactions, the decision about what to capture and post, and assessing whether it reflects your inner self, are processes that can be taken at an individual's pace as he or she prepares and evaluates the self for social media.

Self-judging the fable

Every teen in the study reported engaging in the process of self-assessment to some extent before posting their pictures to Facebook, which may explain why they were so self-aware and reflective in the interviews; they had already done the work to analyze the pictures before they posted them to Facebook. Of course, these teens were aware of their social position and peer judgments at all times, and therefore I do not mean to suggest that they operated outside of social constraints or awareness; however, it is important to note that the work at this point in the creation phase is, at least in some form, done alone. It occurs in the moment they all described in interviews where they look at the picture and make an assessment about the self before posting it. We all do this with any picture we take; we see an image and immediately judge our appearance, actions, or whatever relates to us in the image. The knowledge that this image will be representative of the self in a public discourse, however, makes this work much more powerful than simply doing a quick appearance assessment. This has important implications, both positive and negative, for adolescent development generally and for the sociological understanding of the symbiotic relationship between adolescent development and technology use.

When adolescents like what they see in their images, they affirm the self at that moment, which may positively influence self-esteem. And while peer feedback can also enhance self-esteem, my findings suggest that the internal feedback can be extremely impactful, too. When I asked girls what likes mean to them, they described them fairly generically; girls described likes as showing that "people like you, people think you're pretty or whatever." But, as I mentioned in Chapter 2, because there are so many ways that likes can be interpreted, from the positive—liking something or someone, or just signaling you were there too—to the negative in the form of sarcastic likes, they can be ambiguous. In other words, with likes they know they received some sort of feedback, but they are not always entirely sure what it means. I believe that all this leaves us with statements like "people think you're pretty or whatever." The meaning is there, but it gets discounted a bit along the way.

In contrast, when they see their own picture before they post it, they know exactly what they like about it, and these feelings are powerful. Cassie described the moment when she saw one of her pictures as "if you find one that's really good, you'll be like, 'Oh wow I'm pretty. . .' And like, um, feel good about yourself." She directly links seeing the flattering picture of herself with how she feels about herself. The language "oh wow I'm pretty" is so much more powerful than "people think you're pretty or whatever," used to describe likes. This can extend to pictures that showcase other important aspects of adolescence beyond appearance, such as friendships. I asked Sara about a graduation picture I observed of her with one of her good friends, in which the girls are smiling and hugging. Sara was originally tagged in this picture, but then chose to use it as her profile picture. She said that she "was expecting that it would show up on Facebook so I can see it and have my own copy because that's a picture I wanted to see." While this flattering picture does all the important external work—it signals friendship and attractiveness—Sara does not talk about wanting other people to see this image; instead she talks about how she hoped it would end up on Facebook so that she could see it herself. When she sees the image, she is able to engage in her own assessment feedback loop. And again, her language reflects the power and importance of seeing the image for herself, irrespective of Facebook.

Boys engage in a similar process of self-affirmation, although they are, or at least suggest in the interviews that they are, less focused on affirming appearance and more interested in confirming their masculinity and social belonging in pictures. While several boys mentioned that they are happy to see a flattering picture of themselves, gendered norms encouraged them to downplay this, as Tom did when he pointed out "well it's one of five good pictures ever taken of me." In contrast, they did not downplay how much they loved great sports pictures of themselves and how good it made them feel to see these images. Max spoke about how much cycling came to mean to him when he was transitioning to a new school, and as a result, it was a great boost to his self-story to see pictures of himself "crushing" a century ride in less than three hours. Just seeing the image made him feel like he was part of such an elite group that he was "distancing [himself] from everyone except the people who get it." Although he is comparing himself to the generalizable other (Mead 1962) in this example, seeing the image gives him the "distancing" ability, which was so affirming for him during this uncertain period of school transition.

Myles said that he sees himself as "an awkward teenager who does a lot of sports. . . has a good amount of friends." The awkward comment was not said in a disparaging way; instead he seemed to see it as self-deprecating humor, again confirming the goofy idiot mentality. It is also indicative of the inner dialogue at work, too; he makes sure to note that he is an athlete and has a "good amount of friends." He ends his self-assessment with "I guess dude can handle himself," which highlights his self-confidence. Interestingly, Myles spoke about himself in the third person here, which could be an individual quirk or it could be a sign that he felt more comfortable revealing this rather personal self-assessment by creating a bit of space between his thoughts and statement. He did not clarify what he meant by his ability to "handle himself," but I think he is indicating that in his images he sees himself doing everything he wants to highlight in his Facebook presentation: he asserts masculinity via athletics, is socially connected, follows the Facebook rules, and makes a good presentation. And therefore, he sees himself as someone who has things under control. In some ways, Myles' self-assessment is about his executive functioning skills, likely reflecting norms of traditional masculinity. None of the girls spoke of self-reflecting at this level, but many of the boys used their images and Facebook experiences as indications of their management skills, which appeared to be an esteem boost as well. This suggests that there may be a gendered difference in what gets highlighted for self-assessment as well. Certainly my data illustrates that confirming masculinity and femininity is important for both peer and self-assessment.

Derailment of the self and the inner dialogue

There is potential for positive effects of the self-assessment process when the presentation is authentic and ultimately successful. When individuals cannot produce images that match the self-narrative, the results can be devastating to the evolving sense of self. In Chapters 1–3, I referenced how troubling it can be for teens like Jake when the peer feedback loop does not work out in the ways they hoped, and I think the same can be true for the self-assessment process. Because my participants tended to be fairly effective in their Facebook presentations, I do not have substantial data to draw on here, but will highlight a few examples I observed to illustrate the potentially negative consequences of the inner social media dialogue.

Whenever participants were faced with an image—and this usually happened when they were tagged in images by others—that did not match the inner fable, they reported unease or embarrassment. Charlie's decision to quickly untag himself in the Irish step dancing pictures is a good example of this. Yet, while Charlie was embarrassed initially, it did not have long-term consequences for his sense of self, as the small number of dancing pictures were not his entire presentation. The real danger comes when these images represent the majority of your social media feed. Jake had this problem and tried to navigate it by presenting an inauthentic self. Jake talked about himself as a popular kid and a great basketball player, yet he could not genuinely convey either of these attributes visually on Facebook. His images did not show social connection because he had few pictures with friends and little interaction on his images; he received very few likes, no comments on any images, and only one picture that showed him in a peer context. Additionally, while he had a few basketball pictures, they were mostly off-court or photos of him simply holding a basketball (Figure 4.3), which is not the kind of athletic image other teens captured.

Figure 4.3 Jake's Basketball Picture

This discrepancy leaves Jake stuck. He either has to change his current fable to reflect the images he does have, or he has to stick with his narrative and present a highly edited and perhaps less authentic version of the self. Based on his images, Jake appears to have done the latter, and his Facebook presentation appears stilted. Although this was evident in his current Facebook presentation, apparently his foray onto Facebook in ninth grade went further and he was bullied to such an extent that he was forced to shut down his Facebook. Jake was not overly forthcoming about this time in the interview, but I was able to piece together his story through fragments he shared. The time and energy Jake spent trying to deal with the bullying in ninth grade was evident when he said,

> And then like, I don't know it was just, um, yeah it was just really time consuming. . . And I don't know I just, I kinda was like, I don't think I can control myself, so if I just like, kiboshed it, it's easier than trying to monitor it every day.

I think his description of trying to control himself makes it clear how much effort he put into trying to stop the bullying. Jake was not unaware of the bullying, but in spite of his efforts he could not make it stop. Given the ubiquitous use of

Facebook among his peers at that time, it showed an incredible amount of self-control to remove himself from the technology. It took him four years to return to Facebook, and although his presentation still does not mirror other teens' images, it is a tentative and measured return, one almost completely devoid of any visual presentation of the "real me." He rarely posts, and when he does his postings are often inspirational quotes such as "a smooth sea never made a skilled sailor" that cannot be misinterpreted or used against him. While these posts are beyond the scope of this research, I would argue that his choice of quotations is inherently meaningful for his self-work given his past experiences on Facebook.

What is interesting about Jake's current Facebook presentation is that overall it is a fairly generic presentation with a few meaningful images or quotes sprinkled in at times. While other participants are working boldly at times to present themselves and engage in the self-assessment work, Jake's process has been derailed by his previous Facebook experiences. He cannot really do the self-analysis work I described in the previous sections because he is not fully engaged in his Facebook presentation. Yet how could anyone expect him to assert "this is me now" on Facebook, given his past experiences? This certainly had implications for his sense of self in ninth grade, when the bullying got so bad he felt it was better to "kibosh" Facebook than keep it going. However, I wonder what the implications are for his current Facebook incarnation. If the self-assessment process can lead to benefits such as building confidence and affirming the self, then it is important to note that teens whose experiences have derailed the self-assessment experience not only suffer the negative effects of peer policing, but are also not able to obtain the benefits of the inner dialogic work afforded to their peers.

Jake's narrative pales in comparison to some of the horrible stories in the popular press about the possible links between social media bullying and related suicides and mental health issues (O'Keefe and Clarke-Pearson 2011). But Jake is an interesting example of an adolescent attempting a Facebook redo. He is tentative in his current presentation, and I wonder about the effect of this on his evolving sense of self. If the visible peer and personal feedback loops of social media can build confidence, which can affirm the evolving self, then what happens to Jake, who is not buttressed by the confidence these feedback loops can provide? The data cannot address this question given that Jake was the only example of this in the study, but it is enough to suggest that the consequence of this self-regulation is a derailment of the evolving self, or at the very least, the missed opportunity to do this self-development work.

Notes

1 My focus is on the images, which may be the most thoughtful component, as there is no deadline. It is possible that comments on pictures align more with the brain research because of the norms around immediate response to text on social media.
2 I do think it is possible that this finding would not be as clearly present on some of the disappearing apps such as Snapchat, which are often sent quickly to an individual or group under the assumption that it will disappear after a certain amount of time. I think my comment about the time and effort is connected more to sites like Facebook and Instagram, where they are trying to create a more permanent catalog of pictures of the self.

References

Becker, Howard S. 2003. "New Directions in the Sociology of Art" Paper given at the meeting of the European Sociological Association, Section on the Sociology of Art, Paris, France http://howardsbecker.com/articles/newdirections.html

Boneva Bonka S., Amy Quinn, Robert E. Kraut, Sara Kiesler, and Irina Shklovski. 2006. "Teenage Communication in the Instant Messaging Era" in *Computers, Phones, and the Internet: Domesticating Information Technology*, Oxford series in human-technology interaction, edited by Robert Kraut, Malcolm Brynin, and Sara Kiesler. New York, NY: Oxford University Press.

boyd, danah. 2014. *It's Complicated: The Social Lives of Networked Teens*. New Haven, CT: Yale University Press.

boyd, danah and Nicole Ellison. 2007. "Social Network Sites: Definition, History, and Scholarship" *Journal of Computer-Mediated Communication* 13 (1): 210–230.

Cooley, Charles. 1964. *Human Nature and the Social Order*. New York, NY: Scribner's.

Cooney, Elizabeth. June 28, 2010. "Miracle Grow: The Teen Brain Is a Marvel of Smarts: It's Just Not All Filled in (yet)" *The Boston Globe*.

Davis, Jenny and Nathan Jurgenson. 2011. "Prosuming Identity Online" in *Cyborgology*, edited by Nathan Jurgenson and P. J. Rey. http://thesocietypages.org/cyborgology/

Erikson, Erik H. 1980. *Identity and the Life Cycle*. New York: W.W. Norton & Company.

Goffman, Erving. 1959. *The Presentation of Self in Everyday Life*. New York, NY: Anchor Books, Doubleday.

Holson, Laura. 2014. "Social Media's Vampires: They Text by Night" *New York Times* http://www.nytimes.com/2014/07/06/fashion/vamping-teenagers-are-up-all-night-texting.html?_r=0

John, Nicholas A. 2013. "The Social Logic of Sharing" *The Communication Review* 16 (3): 113–131.

Jurgenson, Nathan and P. J. Rey. 2012. "The Fan Dance: How Privacy Thrives in an Age of Cyber-Publicity" in *Unlike Us Reader: Social Media Monopolies and Their Alternatives*, edited by Geert Lovink and Miriam Rasch. Amsterdam: Institute of Network Cultures.

Kraut, Robert, Michael Patterson, Vicki Lundmark, Sara Kiesler, Tridas Mukophadhyay, and William Scherlis. 1998. "Internet Paradox: A Social Technology That Reduces Social Involvement and Psychological Well-Being?" *American Psychologist* 53: 1017–1031.

Marwick, Alice and danah boyd. 2014. "Networked Privacy: How Teenagers Negotiate Context in Social Media" *New Media and Society* 16 (7): 1051–1067.

Mead, George H. 1962. *Mind, Self, & Society From the Standpoint of a Social Behaviorist*. Edited by Charles W. Morris. Chicago, IL: The University of Chicago Press.

National Institute of Mental Health. 2011. "The Teen Brain: Still Under Construction" NIH Publication No. 11–4929. www.nimh.nih.gov/health/publications/the-teen-brain-still-under-construction/index.shtml

O'Keefe, Gwenn S., Kathleen Clarke-Pearson, and the Council on Communications and Media. 2011. "Clinical Report: The Impact of Social Media on Children, Adolescents, and Families" *Pediatrics* 127: 800–804.

Ruder, Deborah B. September/October 2008. "The Teen Brain" *Harvard Magazine*.

Sunden, J. 2003. *Material Virtualities*. New York: Peter Lang.

Turkle, Sherry. May 7, 2007. "Can You Hear Me Now?" *Forbes Magazine*.

Conclusion
Launching the evolving self

The Facebook presentation of self easily conjures so many sociological frame-works, it feels almost redundant at times. Goffman's (1959) impression manage-ment and front stage performance as well as Cooley's (1964) looking-glass self are natural fits and have been used by many sociologists and social psychologists to explain social media interactions (see Tufecki 2008; Robinson 2007; Walther 2008; Papacharissi 2009; boyd 2007; Hogan 2010; Zarghooni 2007). Similarly, there is data to suggest that social media merely replicates, and some may argue even heightens, a performance of traditional gender scripts (Walther 2008). There-fore, the real critique is whether social media simply replicates the traditional world, albeit in a more visual format. Even with this new technology, is nothing really new?

Adolescents come to social media with many of the friends they already have; while of course they will connect with friends of friends via social media, I would argue that these connections are still rooted in the social networks that exist in their external realities. They basically know the impression they will make with their images, and about how many likes and comments they will receive (and from whom). They know all this because social media is not some online expe-rience that is disconnected from their lives. The teens that I spoke with for this research do not think of themselves as "self splitting" as Turkle (2007, 2011) has described; their lives are lived in multiple social contexts, of which social media is one. However, there is something new in this context. Just as it is a false dichotomy to think of the online and offline as two independent contexts, it is also incomplete to think of these as exactly the same context, just enacted in a different space. The social media technology creates a unique space for self-reflection that differentially impacts teens' development of the self, which I see as an important implication of my research for the field.

During a time in their lives marked by great transitions and developments, ado-lescents are now tasked with presenting the self visually for their peers and, more importantly, for themselves, to see. This is no small task; as Gershon (2010) notes, "virtual communication is a social accomplishment (13)" that we need to recog-nize and appreciate as such. It requires them to manage all the traditional work of adolescence, but also to work to create or curate images to support their story and emphasize the highlights that they want to see and show on social media. In addition, they have to ensure that the presentation is bound within the social and gender rules of the platform as they understand them. And after they have done all this and posted an image, they have to look at this visual representation of the self and contend with feedback from their social media friends and as well as their own assessments of themselves. An incredible amount of self-development work takes place on social media. This work is often dismissed, first because we cannot see much of the work in the curation phase as it is invisible to the viewer, and secondly because, in all honesty, it hard to see any value in another bikini or party picture. Yet in talking to teens, it was clear that almost all of their pictures are important to them and that each serves as "micro-evidence" (Collins 2000), which when taken collectively can have a powerful effect on their path to understanding their self-development.

So much of the power is in the visual; the chance to see a representation of your inner self-narrative on social media, to try to put together literally the story in your mind in a visual highlights reel form, is deeply meaningful for adolescents. When done well (i.e., a presentation that is perceived as authentic and conforms to the social media rules), it can foster a strong self-confidence. It is there in the "wow I am pretty" moments that do not happen for adolescent girls too often offline. This is because while technology has generally sped up every aspect of our society, adolescents can actually use this piece of the social media process to slow down and reflect on their evolving self. To be sure, this not true of the need to like and comment on pictures (Katz and Crocker 2015). I am speaking only about the space at the beginning and end of the process; the time teens have to curate images and reflect on them before posting, and then the time to evaluate the self and peer feedback they receive after posting. These spaces are actually very considered and controlled. The technological affordances of Instagram and Facebook, and the ways in which these teens have co-opted this space, give them the time to reflect on the self in a way that is hard to do in the moment in face-to-face interactions.

The evolving self

This feels like such important and exciting work because the exploration of the self is never completed. The perception of the self can and will change according to experiences (both online and offline) and over time. As a result, the personal fable that adolescents document is the evolving self; it is the image of the self as they conceptualize it in that moment, the real me now. Because the self is evolving gradually, it requires a lot of attention and time. Davis (2014) writes that "a wealth of research shows that despite significant holes in self-knowledge, people readily construct narratives as though their self-knowledge were complete" (17). I love this thinking, as I believe that it offers such insight into how we should think about teens' presentation and the work they do to create it. We may not understand the reasons for or the connections between the image and their story, and indeed they may not always see them either, but the narratives are meaningful to them because they *feel* so real in that moment. The narratives will and should change, with many stops and starts along the way as their knowledge and experiences evolve—adolescence is a messy process—but "this is the real me now"; it feels real and complete in the moment, and I think this speaks to why teens rarely delete their embarrassing younger narratives; they, too, felt true once.

Additionally, the personal fable is now relational. While Elkind (1967), Vartarian (2000), and other personal fable theorists would never argue that one's fable is created in a social vacuum, they did conceive of it as a story that exists for the most part in one's mind. However, posting images that represent aspects of the fable on social media means that to a certain extent, one's story is shared and then reacted to, via comments and likes, by one's peers. In many ways, this makes it a more thoughtful yet vulnerable articulation of the personal fable. The architecture of Facebook and Instagram has allowed us, to use Berger and Luckman's (1967) term, to externalize the personal fable online. This externalization process changes both the construction process and the meaning of the personal fable. Having a visual representation of the personal fable on social media means that it can be accessed repeatedly, at home or with friends, allowing for repeated review and adjustment, and this is the process through which these images become "micro-evidence" (Collins 2000) of the self.

All of these factors help to explain the time and effort these teens spend creating and updating their social media. With the exception of one male participant, everyone spoke about the time they spent gathering images and selecting the ones they would present on social media. When this is coupled with the frequency with which they check social media, it is clear that teens are emotionally invested in this process. This does not diminish the time and energy they devote to their offline presentation, but rather suggests that the online and offline presentations are in constant dialogue, often happening simultaneously, and mutually reinforcing each other through feedback on the personal fable. Importantly though, regardless of whether it occurs on or offline, the development of the personal fable in adolescence is not a linear path that results in the final complete formation of the self. Rather, as mentioned, it is a dynamic process of starts, stops, and changes that evolves as it is repeatedly externalized and internalized over time. The opportunity social media provides to create a visual presentation of that work cannot be underestimated.

The media has tended to fixate on the dangerous implications of the dependence on technology to manage social interactions, especially for teens. Turkle's very popular work (1984, 1995, 2011) has also lent support for a more negative stance on technology's effects on our lives and relationships. Turkle's work in the field, launched 20 years before the creation of Facebook, was prescient and thoughtful, as she was the first to write in a public way about how technology would come to consume so much of our lives and impact our social interactions. And indeed, anyone who observes people in a group, all sitting together but fixated on their phones, can readily accept her hypothesis that we are indeed "alone together" (2011). However, my findings led me to a less uniformly negative conclusion.

I do not think that Turkle is wrong to argue that technology can take away from offline interactions. In the focus groups, I asked questions to address some of Turkle's findings, and the answers revealed support for many of Turkle's concerns. At the time of the study these teens checked social media often, at least several times a day; they report that it is stressful at times (57 percent); they seek to accumulate likes; and they do so by sometimes posting drinking or bikini pictures. Turkle's work serves as a cautionary narrative, warning the reader that adolescents' hypercommitment to technology has diminished their real connections, which for her must take place offline. And quite honestly, the initial focus group data would not present drastically different findings. But to focus on the experiences after a photo has been posted to social media is to reveal only the surface story. My methodology enabled me to analyze teens' Facebook images and talk to them directly about the meanings they make and take from these images.

These findings indicate a need to expand the narrative in the field to account for these quiet, reflective moments that do exist before teens post an image and then again after they receive feedback. Social media has not left younger adolescents confused about friendships, communication, or the self. My participants note that there are times when things happen on social media, such as receiving a like from a "random kid from elementary school," that they do not know what to do with, but for the most part they are pretty clear on where their friendships stand, and they are certainly sure that they have communicated important things about themselves both to their peer audiences and to themselves. The effort teens put into this performance, their awareness of how the performance will land even before the audience sees it, and the desire to present what they perceive to be an authentic self on Facebook all leads me to believe that social media can be an important tool for communicating the self to one's peers.

Teens deserve far more credit for the work they do on social media than we currently give them, and we need to ensure that there is room in the theoretical frameworks to reflect the positive influence of social media's use, whatever it may look like. While the experience is not uniformly positive, at least for those who can follow the rules and execute an accurate performance, using the public space to work through self-development and create an authentic presentation of the self can be powerful.

However, the negative assumptions are warranted for teens like Jake, who have trouble following the rules and end up with a derailed and inauthentic presentation. Negative cases like this one dominate the media coverage. In his interview, Jake's uncertainty was evident; he wondered whether he had communicated effectively with his peers and mentioned that he preferred to engage offline to avoid being misinterpreted. In my sample, Jake's was the lone voice who articulated this narrative. However, most likely in a larger sample there would be more teens like Jake for whom social media is not a powerful and manageable communication tool. This, of course, is an avenue for future research.

Implications for future research

Because visual ethnography of young teens is an emerging method with regards to social media, I believe there is tremendous opportunity for future research. First, it would be interesting to conduct a longitudinal study in which the same methods are used to follow a cohort from early adolescence (age 13–14) to early adulthood (21), to see how the inner dialogue may (or may not) evolve on social media. My research illuminates a few experiences of early adolescence, and the literature in the field focuses primarily on college students, but no one has followed the same cohort throughout adolescence into early adulthood in order to see how the visual fable gets presented and feedback interpreted.

Another obvious avenue for future research would be to recruit more racially and economically diverse participants to see if these findings hold for more non-White, non-middle-class adolescents, and to see whether and how hierarchies shift with intersectional differences. Studying the long-term psychosocial consequences of social media bullying on the development of the self could be very useful as well. I have presented Jake's story here, but I currently have no sense of how representative his experience is or what the long-term effects of his experience may be. Finally, I spoke about how important rule following is for creating a successful Facebook presentation, and as such, I think it would be eye-opening to apply these methods and research questions to adolescents on the autism spectrum, who may have a harder time understanding and implementing the rules. I see tremendous opportunities for social media use with this population, as the technology can take the place of some face-to-face communication; however, there is obviously the risk of significant negative feedback from peers. I believe all of these research projects are viable and would be valuable to pursue in the future.

Study limitations

This work is limited first and foremost by the fact that it is a small in-depth sample and therefore cannot be generalized to describe the adolescent experience as a whole. Participants were largely White, middle-class youths from the northeastern United States, and there is no way to know if their stories, images, and internalization processes are representative of American youth more generally. My hypothesis, based on some differences I noted between the kids in private school and those in urban public schools, is that while the images and rules may change, the processes, particularly the self-work to curate images, will not. But mine is an emerging theory that needs to be more broadly applied to account for differences by race, class, geographic location, and age. Secondly, my study is the first in-depth work in the field on the young adolescent population, and as such, it is challenging to situate their experiences in the larger sociological and social media literature on college students. Much of the literature focuses on late adolescence, which cannot be readily applied to my younger participants, as there is no data to suggest that the experience of college students mimics that of high school teens. Thus, while my data suggests that college experience cannot be used to represent the collective adolescent experience, I cannot really offer a direct critique to any of these findings.

The kids are in control

To quote boyd (2014), "it's complicated" and "the kids are all right," but in addition there is something unique about curating the visual self on social media that provides teens the space and opportunity for self-dialogue that can affirm the evolving of the self. And it is clear to me that these teens are driving this process, both in terms of how they use the technology and how they think about the work they do on social media. Gershon (2010) argues that "how people understand the media they use shapes the ways they will use it" (48). I think that this is true and a point that is important to acknowledge when it comes to teens' social media use. Adolescents use social media in ways that make sense given the definitions and meanings they give to the technology. And in many respects, these meanings and definitions may be different from the ones that adults assign to social media. This book seeks to show at least some of the definitions and meanings that adolescents assign to this technology. This time and space is fostered when they are curating images for Facebook, and this notion forms the basis of my sociological theory of adolescent development and social media. To date, there is very little work in the field that emphasizes the self-reflective process prior to posting. This period of the process is essential for understanding both the adolescents' motivations and the meanings they make of their social media work. I came to this understanding through image analysis and in-depth interviews with the teens. Likes and bikini pictures, I learned, are only one part, the front stage part, of the social media story. The earlier backstage work is just as important for self-development.

This is fundamentally a multidisciplinary study. While it is grounded in the sociological theories of gender and symbolic interactionism, it also considers the ways in which micro interactions and moments of self-reflection can work to constitute the self over time. My research offers media studies a new framework of the multiphased Facebook process, from which to consider the deeper meanings that adolescents make and take from social media. The curation phase work offers an example of a controlled and thoughtful decision-making process that challenges some of the assumptions, based on new brain development research, that adolescents struggle to make good choices. Facebook use can play in the processes of adolescent development. Although Facebook may lose popularity as adolescents move on to the next cool site or platform, social media and, more specifically for this research, the online visual presentation of the self are now a part of our society. The processes that I highlight in this book—creating and curating images, making sense of the feedback they receive online, and using all of this information to evaluate the self—take place on most of the new media we use; indeed, these features are central to Snapchat, which did not exist when I did the interviews for this study. I see no end to the cultural norms around visually documenting the self online. Therefore, while the specific app or site may change, this research can be readily applied to other sites or platforms.

We have only begun to see the effects of this new symbiotic relationship between adolescents and social media technology. In many ways, this relationship has the potential to build self-confidence that can affirm the evolving self and have long-term positive implications for these adolescents. And hopefully, if we can continue to get past our adult judgments of the bikini pictures and bullying, we can continue to engage adolescents in genuine conversations about their experiences and the meanings they are making about the self on social media, an important practical implication of this research. Gopnick (2011), skeptical of the assumption of the negative effects of technology, argues that we have to be able to keep some perspective on youth culture and the notion of the "good ole days" pre-social media. She writes,

> The year before you were born looks like Eden, the year after your children were born looks like Mad Max. . . Is the teenager who comes home from school and IMs her friends while she updates her Facebook page really much worse off than the one who came home and watched *Gilligan's Island* reruns?

My findings suggest that this new generation of digital natives may actually be better off than previous generations of teens who came home and watched television. Instead of mindlessly watching *Gilligan's Island*, these teens are doing some serious presentation and self-development work that unfortunately get masked behind the cliché pictures of adolescence. This relationship is neither a brave new world nor is it a rehash of the same old thing in a different medium. Adolescents are forging a new path to development, and most impressively they are taking control of the technology to do so in a way that has the potential to positively impact their self-development.

References

Berger, Peter L. and Thomas Luckmann. 1967. *The Social Construction of Reality: A Treatise on the Sociology of Knowledge*. New York, NY: Anchor Books.

boyd, danah. 2007. "Why Youth (Heart) Social Network Sites: The Role of Networked Publics in Teenage Social Life" *MacArthur Foundation Series on Digital Learning—Youth, Identity, and Digital Media Volume*, edited by David Buckingham. Cambridge, MA: MIT Press.

———. 2014. *It's Complicated: The Social Lives of Networked Teens*. New Haven, CT: Yale University Press.

Collins, Randall. 2000. "Situational Stratification: A Micro-Macro Theory of Inequality" *Sociological Theory* 18: 17–43.

Cooley, Charles. 1964. *Human Nature and the Social Order*. New York, NY: Scribner's.

Davis, Jenny. 2014. "Triangulating the Self: Identity Processes in a Connected Era" *Symbolic Interaction* 37: 500–523.

Elkind, David. 1967. "Egocentrism in Adolescence" *Child Development* 38: 1025–1034.

Gershon, Ilana. 2010. *Breakup 2.0: Disconnecting Over New Media*. Ithaca, NY: Cornell University Press.

Goffman, Erving. 1959. *The Presentation of Self in Everyday Life*. New York, NY: Anchor Books, Doubleday.

Gopnick, Allison. February 7, 2011. "Diagnosing the Digital Revolution: Why It's So Hard to Tell Whether It's Really Changing Us" *slate.com*. www.slate.com/articles/arts/books/2011/02/diagnosing_the_digital_revolution.html

Hogan, Bernie. 2010. "The Presentation of Self in the Age of Social Media: Distinguishing Performances and Exhibitions Online" *Bulletin of Science, Technology, and Society* 30: 377–386.

Katz, James E. and Elizabeth Thomas Crocker. 2015. "Selfies and Photo Messaging as Visual Conversation: Reports From the United States, United Kingdom and China" *International Journal of Communication* 9: 12.

Papacharissi, Zizi. 2009. "The Virtual Geographies of Social Networks: A Comparative Analysis of Facebook, LinkedIn, and ASmallWorld" *New Media Society* 11: 199–220.

Robinson, Laura. 2007. "The Cyberself: The Self-ing Project Goes Online, Symbolic Interaction in the Digital Age" *New Media Society* 9: 93–110.

Tufecki, Zeynep. 2008. "Can You See Me Now? Audience and Disclosure Regulation in Online Social Networking Sites" *Bulletin of Science, Technology and Society* 28: 20–36.

Turkle, Sherry. 1984. *The Second Self: Computers and the Human Spirit.* Cambridge, MA: MIT Press.

———. 1995. *Life on the Screen: Identity in the Age of the Internet.* New York, NY: Simon and Schuster.

———. May 7, 2007. "Can You Hear Me Now?" *Forbes Magazine.*

———. 2011. *Alone Together: Why We Expect More From Technology and Less From Each Other.* New York, NY: Basic Books.

Vartarian, Lessa Rae. 2000. "Revisiting the Imaginary Audience and Personal Fable Constructs of Adolescent Egocentrism: A Conceptual Review" *Adolescence* 35: 639–661.

Walther, Joseph B. 2008. "The Role of Friends' Appearance and Behavior on Evaluations of Individuals on Facebook: Are We Known by the Company We Keep? *Human Communication Research* 34 (1): 28–49.

Zarghooni, Sasan. Autumn 2007. "A Study of Self-Presentation in Light of Facebook" Institute of Psychology, University of Oslo.

Index

Note: Page numbers in *italics* indicate figures; those in **bold** indicate tables.

Printed in the United States
by Baker & Taylor Publisher Services

Printed in the United States
by Baker & Taylor Publisher Services